Democracy or Republic?

Democracy or Republic?

The People and the Constitution

Jay Cost

AEI PRESS

Publisher for the American Enterprise Institute
WASHINGTON, DC

ISBN-13: 978-0-8447-5051-4 (Hardback)
ISBN-13: 978-0-8447-5052-1 (Paperback)
ISBN-13: 978-0-8447-5053-8 (eBook)

Library of Congress Cataloging in Publication data have been applied for.

AEI PRESS

Publisher for
**American Enterprise Institute
for Public Policy Research**
1789 Massachusetts Avenue, NW
Washington DC, 20036
www.aei.org

Printed in the United States of America

For My Students

Contents

Introduction

The Constitution is the oldest written instrument of government still in effect in the world today. As with so much else in our country, it is polarizing. Conservatives celebrate the Constitution's longevity as a sign of its excellence and encourage Americans to adhere to its basic principles. But lately progressives have grown loud in their critique of the nation's founding charter. Over the past few years, a growing number of writers on the American left has criticized virtually every nook and cranny of our nation's founding charter.

In a December 2020 article for Salon, Greg Coleridge and Jessica Munger asserted that the Constitution is "hopelessly outdated," citing among other maladies "declining public trust," "the electoral crisis," and the COVID-19 pandemic.[1] In a sprawling *Harvard Law Review* essay from November 2020, Michael Klarman lamented the "degradation of democracy" and called for a number of sweeping reforms, including eliminating equal apportionment in the Senate and implementing nationwide multi-member districts determined by ranked-choice voting.[2]

In an October 2019 *Atlantic* article, Sanford Levinson warned readers that the "Constitution *is* the crisis" of our government.[3] (Emphasis in original.) Writing on his Substack page in June 2022, James Fallows bemoaned that "practically no other modern nation still runs on *rules* set up long before the use of electricity, or knowledge of the germ theory."[4] (Emphasis in original.) Appearing on MSNBC's *The ReidOut*, Georgetown Law Professor Rosa Brooks said that Americans "are essentially slaves" to the Constitution, which "was written more than 230 years ago by a tiny group of white slave-owning men."[5]

These criticisms usually boil down to the idea that, far from being a democratic system of government, the Constitution employs a clunky system of checks and balances to prevent the people from ruling. The framers of the Constitution were men of a different era, fearful of popular sovereignty and committed to aristocratic privilege, as embodied by the institution of slavery. But times have changed, opinions have evolved, and the demands of the moment are different. Now, a system of government that leverages the power of the people is needed to institute long overdue policy changes.

This genre is a bit older than today's progressives might appreciate. Writing in the *Atlantic* in the late 19th century, a Princeton academic named Woodrow Wilson compared the American system of government to the British system and found the former lacking in "responsibility." He called for the integration of the executive and legislative branches, to make the American state more responsive to the public.[6] What's more, today's left-wing critique of the Constitution mimics some of the original Anti-Federalist complaints of the Constitution. Anticipating modern progressives, they accused the founders of creating an intentionally confusing system that only had the appearance of a republic, when in fact it was meant to concentrate power in an elite few.

There is something deeply American about calls to reform our system of government. After all, the revolutionary generation did exactly that—twice—first by overthrowing King George III's rule and then by replacing the Articles of Confederation with the Constitution. Some framers can certainly be cited as advocates of periodic, sweeping changes. Thomas Jefferson, for instance, once wrote to James Madison "that the earth belongs in usufruct to the living: that the dead have neither powers nor rights over it."[7] From that, it follows that no generation should be bound by a faulty instrument of government written so long ago.

Too often, the conservative response to the progressive critique can be boiled down to *tough luck*. The founders created a republic, not a democracy. This is hardly a compelling retort. It smacks of the old saw about conservatives liking old things simply because they are old. Progressive columnist Paul Waldman, writing in the *Washington Post* in July 2022, was not entirely wrong when he noted conservatives' tendency to deify the founders, or perhaps their interpretation of the founders: "This is the conceit of today's right: The Founders were essentially perfect, and only we conservatives are capable of interpreting their will."[8]

What is missing from this debate is an understanding of the theory of government embodied by the Constitution. What was the founders' agenda? What was the logic they had in mind? And does that logic suggest a democracy or a republic? What are the differences between these, anyway? All these questions hang in the background of the arguments over the Constitution, but they are rarely addressed directly.

* * * *

It would help to begin this analysis by clarifying some terms. "Democracy" derives from the Greek and means rule by the people. For all intents and purposes, nobody favors an absolute democracy. Most of us think there must be limits. For instance, we generally agree that nobody can have their life, liberty, or property seized without due process of law. Likewise, we generally believe that people have a right to worship God as they please or speak their mind. The existence of these civil rights implies that a democratic government is not allowed to do whatever it wishes and therefore that the rule of the people is not always wise and good.

A republic is not exactly the same as a democracy. The word comes from the Latin res publica, or the public affair. It speaks to the idea that the government belongs to the citizenry and must work on its behalf. The Roman Republic was the first great republic in world history, but the Roman experience illustrates that a republic need not be democratic, strictly speaking. Rome is better understood as an oligarchic republic—in which authority was vested in the citizenry (itself an exclusive subcategory of the population) but tilted toward the wealthy, wellborn, and older. These citizens had greater power in deciding the affairs of the state. Likewise, the Renaissance republics of northern Italy were oligarchic, centralizing power in the hands of the merchants and the large landowners. So also was the Dutch Republic of the early modern era, with power concentrated in the House of Orange.

The United States, on the other hand, was the first democratic republic in the modern world. Citizenship was defined more broadly than any Western nation at the time of the American founding, and distinctions of wealth among citizens were much less significant factors in the distribution of political power. Perhaps Abraham Lincoln offered the best definition of a democratic republic in the Gettysburg Address—"government of the people, by the people, for the people."[9]

Lincoln's statement brings into focus the core tension between republicanism and democracy. What happens when government of the people and by the people is not actually *for* the people? In a simple democracy, the people, or at least a majority of the people, possess supreme power.

If they wield that power for the good of themselves at the expense of the community or the rights of others, it is no longer a democratic republic. It is a democratic tyranny. A democratic republic implies that there must be limits to the majority's power, lest they mistreat the rest of the community.

Even the strongest advocates of democracy believe that individual rights must be protected from majority rule. And virtually all contemporary republicans believe that the people must have meaningful participation in government, as nobody knows the people's interests better than they do. So deep down, all parties to the dispute over the Constitution agree that while democracy is a necessary condition of republicanism, it is not sufficient. The real debate is: Where should the line be drawn? How much democracy is too much?

The Constitution offers a unique theory of democratic republicanism to answer this question. It empowers the people to govern while attempting to redirect the democratic spirit away from dangerous ends. Thus, the progressive critics of the Constitution are correct, in some respects. It is "antidemocratic" in some ways. But the ultimate purpose is to prevent democracy from destroying republicanism.

The central argument of this book is that the Constitution reconciles the occasionally competing values of democracy and republicanism by promoting *consensus in the lawmaking process*. The framers of the Constitution believed that the larger, broader, and more considered a majority is in support of an initiative, the more likely the initiative promotes justice and the general welfare. Such a consensus is not guaranteed to be wise or fair, but the chances are higher than those of a small, narrow, or fleeting majority. The Constitution will usually thwart these in what today we know as "gridlock." This is a feature, not a bug, of our system. Such democratic majorities are potentially dangerous to the republican character of the nation, and thus the Constitution makes it so they struggle to get anything done.

After the law has been crafted, the Constitution builds the executive branch to enforce it with energy and independence from the legislature. It also creates an independent judiciary that is supposed to prize good judgment and wisdom. While these are important features of our governing charter, the emphasis here will predominantly be on the lawmaking process. The enforcement of the law and adjudication of disputes arising under the law are by nature secondary to the creation of the law. There would be little for the president or the courts to do if there were no laws.

The remainder of this book develops in detail the theory that consensus is the underlying principle of the republic. Chapter 1 offers a broad introduction of the historical events that led to the adoption of the Constitution and a brief outline of the contents of our founding charter.

The next five chapters outline the constitutional theory of consensus. Chapter 2 examines how the framers designed a national republic to organize factions in society. Chapter 3 considers how the system of checks and balances was borrowed from the Roman Republic to manage political elites. Chapter 4 brings these considerations into an analysis of the constitutional lawmaking process, which, despite its often byzantine and confusing nature, is designed to promote consensus. Chapter 5 evaluates the trade-offs between a consensus-based regime and a more democratic one, ultimately arguing that the United States can only endure under the former. Chapter 6 delves into the problem of "dead-hand" control, or the notion that the American public is still under the rule of a generation that died more than two centuries ago. While this is true in some respects, it is not true in others and ultimately is not a bad thing for the nation, anyway.

The final three chapters examine challenges to consensus that come from outside the lawmaking process. Chapter 7 considers the peculiar role of political parties, which can facilitate consensus under certain circumstances but in others inhibit it. Chapter 8 critiques the Supreme Court's occasionally heavy-handed role in the lawmaking process. The court's power of judicial review potentially enables it to act as a super legislature, imposing its own views on the body politic. Chapter 9 investigates the role of civic virtue, arguing that while the Constitution does not empower the government to make the people morally good, it does reward a citizenry that appreciates the value of compromise.

This book is not intended as a top-to-bottom defense of the Constitution. The focus is, rather, on how the lawmaking process as outlined by the Constitution resolves the tensions between a democracy and a republic through the idea of consensus. Aspects of our government that are not directly related to this process, such as federalism, do not get much treatment here. Likewise, there are many ways that the law can make consensus more or less likely, but they are not considered here because the emphasis is on the Constitution. The sweeping power of the bureaucracy, for instance, is of enormous relevance to the question of consensus in a democratic republic, but the bureaucracy is the creation of the law, rather than the Constitution. Likewise, the matter of campaign finance is of great importance to the question of consensus but is not considered here because it is also a product of the law.

It will come as no surprise, as you read through these pages, that I am a deep admirer of the nation's governing charter. At a minimum, my hope is that readers will appreciate that there is a logic to the Constitution. It may be old. It may have been created by a bunch of "white slave-owning men."[10] But it makes sense. The framers did not toss it together at random. They had a purpose to it. And before we dismiss the document out of hand or call for drastic reforms, we at least need to appreciate that purpose. They understood that while democracy was necessary for the survival of the republic, it could potentially be a destructive force. It had to be contained. In offering a solution to this problem, the Constitution remains a substantial achievement in political philosophy. If it does not deserve our reverence, it at least deserves our understanding.

1

The Basics

At most colleges and universities, the framers of the US Constitution are not really studied in courses on political philosophy. Students will read Plato and Aristotle, Thomas Hobbes and John Locke, and Jean-Jacques Rousseau and Karl Marx. But usually they will not read James Madison or Alexander Hamilton, at least not past the Federalist Papers, the essays composed largely by those two to defend the Constitution. And even then, only a handful of these essays will probably be assigned. Beyond that, students will not encounter Rufus King, John Dickinson, Gouverneur Morris, James Wilson, or any of the other major contributors to the Constitutional Convention, unless they take a graduate seminar on the subject.

This is, in part, a consequence of the faddishness of higher education. The framers are just not "in" at the moment. But it is also because the authors of the Constitution were not philosophers, as we understand the term today. A few were essayists, no doubt. Hamilton in particular wrote frequently for the newspapers under various pseudonyms. But none put together any systematic theory of politics. Madison never bequeathed to the world a *Politics*, as Aristotle did.[1] George Mason never wrote his version of Locke's *Second Treatise of Government*.[2]

It is better to say the framers were Enlightenment men of politics. Politics was the great American pastime of the 18th century, a consequence of its colonial development. Under the mercantile system, the British restricted what kinds of enterprises the Americans could undertake, so that they would never compete with British manufacturers or merchants. This limited the career prospects of enterprising men in the middle and upper echelons of American society and drove them toward the bar or the pulpit. As Edmund Burke said of America during a speech in the House of Commons, "In no country perhaps in the world is the law so general a study. The profession itself is numerous and powerful; and in most provinces it takes the lead."[3] This contributed to the mastery of many political skills—reasoning, rhetoric, and argumentation—and a keen understanding of how a just and fair government should function. And because the British monarch was content to leave the colonies alone for the first half of the 18th century, the Americans were largely free to govern themselves.

The Enlightenment was the dominant intellectual movement in the West between the 17th and 19th centuries. The American Revolution occurred right around the middle of this. It was a time of confidence in man's capacity to learn. Isaac Newton's *Principia Mathematica* introduced a series of mathematical equations that seemed to explain the entire physical universe.[4] Francis Bacon's *Novum Organum* detailed what we today call the scientific method for acquiring new knowledge.[5] The study of politics had also become a kind of science. Hobbes's *Leviathan* and Locke's *Second Treatise of Government* employed rational principles to understand how a state should be organized.[6] In the same year as the American Revolution, Adam Smith published the *Wealth of Nations*, which used scientific ideas to make sense of the realm of economics. It appeared that reason and science could apprehend the entirety of existence.[7]

Americans of wealth and status often had their children educated in an astonishing array of this knowledge, not just from the Enlightenment but dating all the way back to classical antiquity. Madison and Thomas Jefferson, both born to affluent families, received such an education. They spoke multiple languages, including Greek and Latin; knew the ancient historians and philosophers backward and forward; read the modern theories of Locke and Montesquieu; applied techniques of scientific agriculture to their plantations; and more. Jefferson even taught himself architecture and designed Monticello, his famous homestead, and the Academical Village at the University of Virginia.

Jefferson's lifelong passion for architecture is an analogy for the relationship between the framers and political philosophy. He wrote no great treatise on architecture, but the buildings he designed blended classical styles with modern realities in ingenious ways. So it was with the framers. None ever wrote a book-length work on political philosophy. Rather, the US Constitution embodies their ideas on politics. It was their contribution to the conversation that had been ongoing among thinkers since classical antiquity.

Ironically, none of them intended this to be their life's great achievement. Most were born during the reigns of George I (1714–27) or

George II (1727–60), a period of harmony between Great Britain and its American colonies. The affection the colonists had for their sovereigns was reflected in the names of cities, towns, and institutions in colonial Virginia: the College of William and Mary, King and Queen County, Queen Anne County, King George County, Orange County, Williamsburg, and Hanover County. In 1760, when George III ascended to the British throne, no serious person could possibly have imagined that the colonists would form their own nation less than 20 years later.

Nevertheless, between 1763 and 1776, the Americans moved in fits and starts toward a decisive break from Great Britain. After the French and Indian War, Great Britain was in debt and demanded the colonies help pay it off through taxes. When the colonies resisted, the British government began violating what the Americans took to be their sacred rights as Englishmen—the right to have new taxes approved by their representatives, the right to trial by jury, and even the right to be governed by their colonial charters. Starting with the Sugar Act in 1763, which imposed a tax on sugar, and culminating with the Intolerable Acts of 1773, which placed Boston under martial law, George III had proven to the colonists that he was intent on governing as an absolute monarch. In 1776, the colonists formally declared their independence, and the United States of America was born.

For us today, it is exciting to look back on this period of our history. But this was a perilous moment—both militarily and politically. The Americans had to not only battle the most powerful Western nation but also create an entirely new system of government.

* * * *

The Americans had read the great works of the Western canon, but they had all been written by Europeans dealing with the unique problems their civilization faced. Modern European thinkers were grappling with the legacy of medievalism—an essentially static society, divided among those who fought (the nobility), those who prayed (the clergy), and those who worked (the peasants). They were struggling to liberate Europe from what historians have called the "great chain of being," whereby everybody was born into their place and owed deference to those above them.[8]

This was nothing like the American experience. America had no class of nobles. A large portion of the white male population owned land, whereas in Europe, tenant farming was still widespread. As for those white men who did not own land, the unsettled western territory beckoned with immense opportunities for upward mobility. Moreover, the Americans had relatively little by way of a commercial or craft-oriented middle class, which meant no European-style guild structure to stratify them. America did not even have large cities, certainly not compared to the booming metropolises of Paris or London. Boston, New York, and Philadelphia would have been second-tier cities at best in most European nations.

Culturally, there were great dissimilarities between Americans and Europeans. Literacy rates were higher in the United States than in the Old World. And the American civil discourse was wide-ranging, robust, and unregulated. The legacy of John Peter Zenger loomed large. Zenger, a newspaper printer who was charged with libel in 1734 for criticizing the royal governor of New York, was acquitted by a jury of his colonial peers—effectively establishing that the Americans would abide no limits on what they say or write about their rulers. Nobody was afraid of speaking their mind, at least not after George III was deposed.

American Christianity was likewise profoundly different from the European model, in which a centralized ecclesiastical authority reigned supreme—the Catholic Church in most of continental Europe or the Anglican hierarchy in Great Britain. American Christianity, on the other hand, was decentralized and diverse. While some states had established churches, most had separated the church from politics by the time the Constitution was drafted. And in those places where the church still was officially established, its influence in government was waning. Even the tenor and tone of worship was different in America. During the Great Awakening of the 18th century, American Protestantism was reimagined as a lively and democratized faith, quite apart from the staid traditions of Europe.

These many differences between the two civilizations meant that the founders could take what they found interesting or relevant from a European philosopher and discard the rest. As historian Carl Richard put it:

> The founders wandered the unmarked borderlands between
> classical republicanism and liberalism, scavenging for building

materials. The specific materials selected on each foray depended upon the nature of the problem at hand and upon the mood of the scavenger, which helped determined the scavenger's perception of the nature of the problem.[9]

Perhaps the best example of the American penchant for creative use of the European tradition comes from the differences between Jefferson and Locke. Jefferson's most famous claim in the Declaration of Independence— "We hold these truths to be self-evident, that all men are created equal, that they are endowed by their Creator with certain unalienable Rights"— was inspired by Locke's *Second Treatise of Government*, which argued that humans create government as a contract to preserve their rights.[10] In doing so, Locke asserted, people leave what he called the "state of nature," a place of perfect liberty without any government. To European readers, this must have seemed like a place lost to prehistory, but to the Americans, it described their own experience settling the New World. And whereas Locke used his theory to justify replacing the Catholic James II on the English throne with the Protestant William III, Jefferson repurposed Locke's ideas to call for the elimination of monarchy itself.

The European philosopher whose ideas were most directly relevant to the American experience was Charles de Secondat, baron de Montesquieu— or, more simply, Montesquieu. A member of the French aristocracy from Bordeaux, Montesquieu published *The Spirit of the Laws* in 1748. A sprawling masterwork of moral and political philosophy, it set aside abstract reasoning about politics to ground its assertions in historical and cultural facts. Colonial Americans ate Montesquieu up and considered his judgments as almost divinely inspired, for it seemed as though he was speaking straight to them.

A few of Montesquieu's ideas became particularly entrenched in the American intellectual milieu. First, he unequivocally praised the British system of government for its separation of power into three parts—the Parliament, which writes the law; the king, who enforces it; and the courts, which adjudicate it. He believed that separating these functions of government kept power from being abused and thus secured at least the potential for liberty. Montesquieu's analysis of the British system was, to say the least, highly stylized—and more of a description of what some British intellectuals thought their system should be than what it really was. Still, the American colonial governments were modeled on the British notion of separated powers, so Americans saw Montesquieu's praise of the British system as a validation of their own governments.

Second, Montesquieu had good news to share with the Americans about the kind of democratic republic they were looking to build. He believed that such regimes should be small and depended on virtuous citizens who put the good of their community ahead of themselves. In a passage that no doubt resonated with many Americans, Montesquieu wrote:

> In a large republic, there are large fortunes, and consequently little moderation in spirits; the depositories are too large to put in the hands of a citizen; interests become particularized; at first a man feels he can be happy, great, and glorious without his homeland, and soon, that he can be great only on the ruins of his homeland. . . . In a large republic, the common good is sacrificed to a thousand considerations; it is subordinated to exceptions; it depends upon accidents. In a small one, the public good is better felt, better known, lies nearer to each citizen; abuses are less extensive there and consequently less protected.[11]

It seemed to the Americans that Montesquieu was offering a perfect description of the 13 American states *as they were*. They were reasonably compact political units—not as small as the Greek city-states but still fairly small. And the Americans thought themselves quite virtuous, free of the corruption they believed pervaded British politics. In fact, many political theorists over the centuries had argued that the greatest storehouse of civic virtue was the independent farmer, the very sort that constituted the bulk of the American citizenry in 1776.

If a large republic is threatened by "internal vice," as Montesquieu wrote, then a small republic could meet its end "by a foreign force." Often lacking economic might or a large population to defend itself against powerful empires, small republics face constant threats. The solution, Montesquieu argued, was a "federal republic" or "an agreement by which many political bodies consent to become citizens of the larger state that they want to form."[12] So long as all the members of the federation have the same basic type of government, such systems are sustainable.

The Americans dutifully followed Montesquieu's suggestion. In 1777, the Continental Congress adopted the Articles of Confederation, a loosely organized government that depended on a "firm league of friendship" among the 13 states.[13] It was a disaster. The Articles of Confederation may have had the form of a government, but it lacked the substance of one. Admittedly born of the crisis of the moment, but completely incapable of meeting it, it was undone a decade later and unlamented thereafter.

* * * *

There were many serious flaws with the Articles of Confederation. For starters, there was no executive or judicial branches, just the Continental Congress. All governments had to be able to effectuate their will, but without an executive or courts, Congress could not do that. It depended on the state governors and courts, which often ignored its laws. Congress also lacked many essential powers, above all the authority to tax. It relied on the states to supply what were called "requisitions," but the states typically failed to pay. Congress was left to pay for the war by printing money, which generated an ever-worsening cycle of inflation.

None of this seemed like it would cripple the revolution, at least at first. The year 1776 was generally a good one for the American war effort. The Patriots had cleared the British from Boston, and while they had lost New York City, George Washington's army escaped mostly intact and won a symbolic victory at Trenton on Christmas that year. The year 1777 brought the triumph of Saratoga, when British Gen. John Burgoyne was forced to surrender his entire army to Americans Horatio Gates and Benedict Arnold. That victory helped convince the French to join the war effort, and Benjamin Franklin, then serving as an American minister to France, secured the Franco-American alliance in 1778.

Yet 1779 saw no decisive break for the Americans, but rather the beginning of a transition in British strategy. Abandoning their previous effort to cut New England off from the rest of the states, the British turned southward, capturing Georgia in 1779 and Charleston in 1780. Congress tasked Gates with rebutting the British southern assault, but his army was routed at the Battle of Camden. Adding insult to injury, Arnold betrayed the country and nearly succeeded in his conspiracy to hand West Point to the British. Meanwhile, without a reliable source of taxes and beset with hyperinflation, Congress struggled to supply and compensate the soldiers.

It was out of this debacle that a group of nationalists would emerge. Some, like Washington, were inside the military. Others, like Madison, were in Congress. They believed that if the American experiment in liberty were to succeed, the nation would need a competent government. Despite their efforts, the states remained stubbornly committed to retaining their sovereignty and refused to strengthen congressional power.

If the war had dragged on much beyond 1780, who knows what would have happened to the Articles of Confederation. It clearly was not fit for the task of governance. But the Americans began to catch some breaks by the end of that year. The British had hoped to recruit southern loyalists, but to little avail. Then in October, British forces under Lord Cornwallis lost at Kings Mountain. Gates had been replaced by the more capable Nathaniel Greene, who defeated Cornwallis at Cowpens in January. While Cornwallis won a tactical victory at the Battle of Guilford Courthouse in March, it came at heavy casualties. Meanwhile, the guerilla efforts in South Carolina from the famous Francis Marion (the "Swamp Fox," portrayed by Mel Gibson in the movie *The Patriot*[14]) reduced the British foothold in South Carolina and enabled Greene's army to effectively take it back by June 1781.

By this point, Cornwallis had moved to occupy Yorktown, in southern Virginia. After word came that Adm. François Joseph Paul de Grasse, commanding a French fleet, would sail to North America from the Caribbean, Washington furiously marched his army southward, hoping to trap Cornwallis at Yorktown. The plan succeeded, and in October 1781, the British commander had no choice but to surrender his entire army to the combined Franco-American forces. The stunning defeat at Yorktown reverberated across the Atlantic, and public support in Great Britain for the war basically collapsed.

Yorktown marked the end of combat with the British, but it also destroyed the prospect of fixing the government. The nationalist moment was born from the crisis of 1780. By the winter of 1781–82, the crisis was over, as was the imperative for reform. The underlying problems, however, remained. The Articles of Confederation were simply not up to the challenges of running a country like the United States.

Matters grew worse after the war. The Treaty of Paris, which formally ended the Revolutionary War, was a remarkably good deal for the United States. The American delegation, under the direction of New York diplomat John Jay, acquired most of the present-day United States east of the Mississippi River. In return, the Americans made only a few, modest pledges—particularly to pay back debts to British merchants and respect the rights of those Americans who had stuck with Great Britain during the war. But these "loyalists," as they were known, were an easy target for state governments. Seizing loyalist property meant that states did not have to raise taxes on everybody else. Because Congress lacked the power to enforce the treaty, it was unable to stop these violations. The British used them as a pretext to retain forces in the west, where there was money to be made off the fur trade with the Native Americans.

The states also became commercial rivals. After the war, America resumed trade with Great Britain, which created new opportunities for taxes on imported goods. But since Congress could not levy taxes, the states implemented tariffs for their own interests. That led to conflict. If New York raised tariff rates to take advantage of the commercial traffic flowing to New York City, New Jersey would lower its rates to draw trade in its direction. This competition played into the hands of British merchants, who could pick and choose the best place to ship their goods.

Just as they undermined the national interest, the states also mistreated their own citizens. The most dangerous antagonism was between rich and poor. The end of the war brought about a nasty recession that left many small farmers deeply in debt and clamoring for relief. Rhode Island inflated debts away by printing its own currency, outraging creditors in neighboring Boston. Massachusetts, where the merchant class dominated the government, not only denied debt relief to farmers but shifted a greater share of the tax burden onto them. In 1786, local protests turned violent, and soon a full-blown rebellion was under way, led by Capt. Daniel Shays, a veteran of the Revolutionary War. The rebels began seizing courthouses, effectively overthrowing the local governing authority. Meanwhile, Gov. John Hancock seemed helpless to stop it.

The uprising frightened wealthy landowners, merchants, and middle-class people throughout the nation. This was the moment many Americans awakened to the fact that their country was falling apart. For

10 years, the Americans had given a fair test of Montesquieu's theory of a confederation of republics, and it had not worked. The weak central government could barely wage war and failed to hold the states together. The state governments made a mockery of the idea that Americans possessed the selfless virtues that Montesquieu thought necessary to sustain a free society.

Worse, with Montesquieu's vision of a confederation of small republics having failed, the Americans could derive no direct guidance from any European intellectuals. Indeed, if any ideas seemed to have special relevance to the American experience, it was perhaps those of Polybius, the ancient historian whose *Histories* chronicled the rise of the Roman Republic. Drawing on Plato and Aristotle, Polybius argued that there were three types of government—of the one, of the few, and of the many—that could either govern for the good of all (monarchy, aristocracy, and a republic, respectively) or the good of itself (despotism, oligarchy, and mob rule, respectively). Polybius then sketched out a process of development, apogee, and decay, whereby each of the good forms of government was inevitably corrupted into its unjust twin until finally replaced by the next form. So monarchy gives way to despotism; and then to aristocracy, oligarchy, republicanism, and mob rule; and then back to square one. This "regular cycle," he said, occurred according to a "natural order" that occurs again and again in human civilization.[15]

Americans who had read the *Histories* must have felt an eerie similarity between Polybius's theory and their experience.[16] When George III was crowned king in 1760, the colonists celebrated the reign of a just and benevolent monarch. Sixteen years later, they denounced him as a despot and set about making a republic. Now it seemed with Shays's Rebellion that the republic was on the verge of collapsing into mob rule. Perhaps America was caught in a tragic cycle of its own. And what was next? Would it fall into civil war? Would it return to the orbit of the European powers? Would an American despot rise to dominate it?

The good news, at least from Polybius's perspective, was that the Roman Republic had managed to arrest this tragic cycle through its constitution. The Romans had done this, Polybius noted, by "continually adopting reforms from knowledge gained in disaster."[17] Now that disaster had struck the Americans, the question was whether they could do likewise.

Americans were resolved to try, at the least. In March 1787, the Continental Congress called for a convention to "revise" the Articles of Confederation and "render the federal constitution adequate to the exigencies of government and the preservation of the Union."[18] This meeting came to be known as the Constitutional Convention. This was the best chance since 1780 to fix the political problems that ailed the United States, but it might very well have been the *last* chance. If the delegates had failed, the country might indeed have fallen apart.

One can get a sense of the mood of national crisis by noting who attended the Constitutional Convention. The states sent their most eminent men. Washington and Franklin were bona fide international celebrities. Robert Morris of Pennsylvania and Dickinson of Delaware were known throughout the country. Men like William Paterson of New Jersey, John Rutledge of South Carolina, and William Samuel Johnson of Connecticut were well respected in their own states. Many younger men who would go on to achieve great fame were also present; Madison of Virginia and Hamilton of New York were first among them. But Oliver Ellsworth of Connecticut, King of Massachusetts, and Morris of Pennsylvania would have important careers in government thereafter.

From May to September 1787, they met at what we today know as Independence Hall in Philadelphia. They debated, argued, bargained, and ultimately compromised their way to the US Constitution. The fruits of their labor would change the course of world history. At the end of the Constitutional Convention, Franklin noted that the woodworking on the president's armchair depicted a half sun on it and saw it as an analogy for the Constitution:

> I have . . . often in the course of the Session, and the vicissitudes of my hopes and fears as to its issue, looked at that behind the President without being able to tell whether it was rising or setting: But now at length I have the happiness to know that it is a rising and not a setting Sun.[19]

More than two centuries later, it is evident that Franklin's prophecy has proven true. Let's pause the historical narrative to review just what the framers accomplished.

* * * *

The Constitution is not a hard read. Its prose is straightforward and crisp, and it gets directly to the point. It is seven articles long, about the length of a chapter in a book. The first three articles create the legislative, executive, and judicial branches, respectively. The remaining four articles deal with various issues such as relations among the states, amendments, and ratification.

Article I establishes two chambers of Congress, the House of Representatives and the Senate, which together form the supreme lawmaking body in the government. For laws to be passed, both the House and the Senate must enact the same bill. Each chamber is independent of the other. The House has total say over how the House is run, and the Senate is likewise the master of its own rules. The chambers also have unique powers, although the Senate's are more meaningful. All tax bills must originate in the House (in practice, the Senate often writes tax laws), and the House has the sole power to impeach civil officers. Meanwhile, the Senate has the authority to ratify treaties, approve presidential appointments to the executive and judicial branches, and conduct trials to determine whether officers impeached by the House should be removed.

Congress cannot pass any law it wants. Article I, Section 8 of the Constitution enumerates its powers, so if an authority is not listed or at least implied there, Congress does not have the capacity to do it. Over the past 30 years, the Supreme Court has struck down several pieces of legislation on the grounds that Congress lacked constitutional authority. Congressional power is specifically limited in some ways in Section 9. This "mini" bill of rights includes a prohibition against bills of attainder (laws declaring some group or individual to be illegal) and ex post facto laws (laws declaring a previously legal action as now being susceptible to criminal charges). The Bill of Rights, adopted after the Constitution was ratified, further limits congressional power.

The House of Representatives is elected directly by the people for two-year terms. The idea was that the House would reflect public opinion as closely as possible. The Senate, on the other hand, was supposed to be more distant from the ebbs and flows of the public mood. Senators were originally chosen by state legislatures to serve for six-year terms. The

17th Amendment, ratified in 1913, established the direct election of senators, giving the public greater control over the chamber. House seats are apportioned to states based on population, with each state getting at least one. Today, the average House seat has about 750,000 people.[20] On the other hand, apportionment in the Senate is equal among the states, with each getting two senators regardless of population.

Article II creates the executive branch, headed by the president. The framers had considered an executive commission but decided that the executive power is best wielded by a single person. The president is responsible for making sure the laws are faithfully executed, and the First Congress decided that this meant he had the power to fire his administrators, even though such a power is not expressly mentioned in the Constitution. He has the power to nominate executive and judicial officials, but his nominations must receive the approval of the Senate. Likewise, he has the power to negotiate treaties, but he must get the assent of the Senate before they have the force of law.

The president also has a role in domestic legislation. He can veto bills he does not like or that he thinks are unconstitutional, but Congress can override his veto with a two-thirds vote of both the House and Senate. He can call Congress into special session, a power reserved traditionally for emergencies, and he is obligated to provide them with information regarding what the Constitution calls the State of the Union. Today, the president gives a long, campaign-style address, but for much of the country's history, the president submitted a written report to Congress on the condition of the country.

To choose the president, the framers created the Electoral College, an often-misunderstood institution that was the product of necessity. The framers wanted the president to be independent of Congress; therefore, he could not be chosen by it. They were also concerned that the people did not have the necessary wisdom to select the best person for the job. The Electoral College emerged as a compromise. Each state would get electors equal to its total House and Senate seats, and the state legislatures would decide how they were distributed among presidential candidates. To become president, a candidate would have to win a majority of electors. If no candidate crossed this threshold, the House would choose from among the top three finishers. The process did not work very well, however, and within a generation, most states would award their electors to the candidate who won the popular vote in the state.

Article III establishes the courts, although it does not say much about what they will look like. The Americans had bad experiences with royal courts before the revolution, as George III used them to abuse colonial rights. So the framers mainly left the details to Congress, making Article III much shorter than Articles I or II. Importantly, Article III grants the Supreme Court the power to arbitrate disputes arising under the laws and the Constitution. In 1804, the Supreme Court under Chief Justice John Marshall would use this rather vague phrasing to establish the power of judicial review, in which the Court has the final say on the meaning of the Constitution.

Article IV governs relations among the states. They must give full faith and credit to the public documents of one another, and they must treat citizens of other states the same as they treat their own. This article also gives Congress the power to add new states and obliges Congress to guarantee every state a republican form of government.

Article V details the amendment process. Two-thirds of Congress can propose an amendment to the state legislatures, of which three-quarters are required to ratify it, thus adding it to the Constitution. Alternatively, two-thirds of the state legislatures can call another constitutional convention, and its recommendations likewise take effect with three-fourths of the states in agreement.

Article VI establishes that the new government will pay the debts contracted under the Articles of Confederation, that US laws shall be supreme over state laws, that public officers in the states and the federal government must swear an oath of allegiance to the Constitution, and that a religious test for assuming office is illegal. Article VII establishes that the agreement of nine of the 13 states will be sufficient for the Constitution to take effect for the states that have agreed to it.

* * * *

When they finished their work on September 17, 1787 (which we today celebrate as Constitution Day), the delegates sent the proposed government to the Continental Congress, which then forwarded it to the states. But it was not the state governments that would approve or reject it, but rather special ratifying conventions, chosen by the citizenry. One reason the delegates at the Constitutional Convention selected this route was that, since the Constitution would govern the people directly, it should have their approval. Another was that, since the Constitution redistributed power from the states to the new national government, the state governments were likely to be greater skeptics. Better to give it to the people.

The ratification debates of 1787 through 1788 were the first truly national event in American democracy. In 12 of the 13 states, voters selected delegates to attend these ratifying conventions. (Rhode Island, which had not sent delegates to the Constitutional Convention, instead held a popular plebiscite, which rejected it.) The first state to ratify was Delaware, and it did so overwhelmingly. Then, in quick succession came Pennsylvania and New Jersey.

But skepticism was building. In the fall of 1787, a series of anonymous essays began to appear in the press denouncing the Constitution in strident terms. Essays by authors such as "Brutus," "Federal Farmer," and "Centinel" argued that the Constitutional Convention had violated the most fundamental maxims of free government. The Anti-Federalists (as they became known) asserted that true republics had to be small and closely tied to the people. This new form of government looked to them like a would-be oligarchy. Distant from the people, it would fall under the sway of the wealthy and wield such massive powers that it would crush the states. Some even suggested that it was all part of a plot by the rich to exploit panic over Shays's Rebellion to destroy liberty.

To counter these attacks, Hamilton and Madison (with occasional contributions from Jay) authored the Federalist Papers. In a series of 85 essays published between October 1787 and December 1788, they laid out in plain language the case for the Constitution. These essays were originally published in New York newspapers and probably had little direct impact, for the New York ratifying convention was stocked with Anti-Federalists. But advocates of the Constitution shared the essays with one another, and the ideas spread throughout the 13 states, helping allay fears that the Constitution would undermine the republic.

The Federalist Papers are an intellectual triumph and our most important resource for understanding the framers' view of the Constitution. But ratification was no guarantee. As 1787 rolled into 1788, Georgia and

Connecticut easily adopted the new charter, bringing the total to five states. But it hit a snag in Massachusetts, where some high-profile revolutionaries—above all Samuel Adams and Hancock—were skeptical. In December 1787, Adams wrote to Richard Henry Lee of Virginia (himself an opponent of the Constitution), "I confess, as I enter the Building I stumble at the Threshold. I meet with a National Government, instead of a Federal Union of Sovereign States."[21]

Still, there was a general sense among the delegates to the Massachusetts convention that something had to be done, as their state had endured the anarchy of Daniel Shays and his rebels. Ultimately, the delegates brokered a compromise. Massachusetts would adopt the Constitution as is, with no strings attached, and then would submit a list of proposed amendments to the new Congress, outlining ways the document could be improved. By the end of July 1788, Maryland, South Carolina, New Hampshire, Virginia, and New York had all followed the same strategy, ratifying the Constitution and recommending amendments. North Carolina ratified in the fall of 1789, while Rhode Island held out until May 1790.

The Bill of Rights was mainly put together by Madison during the First Congress, to make good on this compromise. He drew on the recommendations of the states and older sets of rights such as the Virginia Declaration of Rights of 1776 and the English Bill of Rights of 1689. Congress proposed 12 amendments to the states in fall 1789, and 10 were ratified by December 1791. Since then, there have been just 17 amendments beyond the original Bill of Rights. Considering all the changes in government the world has seen since the Constitution was adopted, our system of government has proven remarkably durable.

2

A National Republic

In a letter to George Washington written in the spring of 1787, James Madison lamented the failure of the Articles of Confederation. The government had not done its two most fundamental tasks: securing justice and promoting the general welfare. But what should replace it? Madison was still thinking this question through. The great necessity in a republican government, he told Washington, "which has not yet been found," was "some disinterested [and] dispassionate umpire in disputes" between the different factions in society. The Americans knew from the tyranny of George III that a monarch is no solution to check the people. As Madison argued, even though the king may be "more neutral to the interests and views of different parties . . . he too often forms interests of his own repugnant to those of the whole." Also, as the decade under the Articles of Confederation had demonstrated, a democratic republic organized along the lines suggested by Montesquieu was also a problem, because, per Madison, the "majority who alone have the right of decision, have frequently an interest . . . in abusing it."[1]

Madison was getting at something we might call *the essential problem of government*. Even though human beings are aware that justice is a necessary precondition for society, they are not capable of spontaneously producing it. They cannot put aside their personal interests for the sake of the public interest, and they often confuse their own desires for the good of the community. The job of government is to do what people individually cannot. It serves as a "dispassionate umpire" that will arbitrate disputes between people, produce justice, and ultimately enable social flourishing. The problem is that government—whether it be a democracy, a monarchy, or something in between—is run by human beings. So even as government is created to secure justice, it can easily become the principal agent of injustice. This is what Madison was getting at in his famous quotation from *Federalist* 51. "If men were angels, no government would be necessary. If angels were to govern men, neither external nor internal controls on government would be necessary."[2]

As men of the Enlightenment, Madison and the rest of the framers believed that while the essential problem of government could not be solved, the emerging science of politics could minimize its bad effects. That is what they tried to do in the Constitution, whose foundational principle is the idea of *consensus*. As they had seen under the Articles of Confederation, democratic majorities can act selfishly, enriching themselves at the expense of the entire community or the rights of others. But the framers believed that the larger, broader, and more considered a majority becomes, the more likely its views are in the public interest. So, the framers sought to empower those sorts of coalitions to rule while trying to thwart smaller, narrower, and more fleeting majorities.

This points to the framers' *worldview*. Worldviews are systems of belief that explain how the world and everything in it, including human beings, relate to one another. Everybody by necessity relies on a worldview, whether they acknowledge it or not. Governments are likewise built on worldviews, for every government is founded on beliefs about how its subjects relate to each other and the state. To understand what motivated the framers and really appreciate why consensus was their method of securing good government, we need to know something about their worldview and how it influenced the Constitution. When we do, we discover they had a great skepticism about humanity's potential for goodness or wisdom, and they reckoned that the most rational way to create a just government was to emphasize compromise between different factions of society.

* * * *

Today we live under a Constitution committed to the protection of individual rights. We take this for granted as just "the way things are done." Yet when we examine earlier civilizations, we see how we hold beliefs about the world that people in the past did not. The Greek philosopher Aristotle, for instance, believed that the ideal life was one of eudaemonia, or excellence lived according to the precepts of virtue. He also believed that because human beings are by their nature social animals, the government played a role in bringing about eudaemonia. In the Middle Ages, scholastic philosophers such as Thomas Aquinas read Aristotle through the lens of medieval Catholicism to argue that church and state are together responsible for the salvation of souls, which justified the punishment of death for heretics who refused to recant their errors.

Such a position is antithetical to the view embodied by our Constitution. The job of the state is not to make us better people, let alone save our souls. Beyond protecting our rights and promoting physical security—food, housing, and medical care—the government leaves us alone, to either flounder or flourish. While Aquinas would put heretics to death, the First Amendment strictly prohibits the government from taking sides in religious disputes.

The Constitution enshrines other views about the world, like the idea that popular sovereignty is the only source of legitimacy for the state—hence the phrase that opens the Constitution, "We the People of the United States."[3] Again, this was different for much of human history, when sovereigns claimed the right to rule by conquest, heredity, or divine sanction.

While the worldview of the Constitution is anchored in popular sovereignty, it also includes an underlying skepticism about the people's ability to wield power responsibly. The framers of the Constitution were at great pains to channel the public energies away from destructive ends. This is different from many modern nations, where most governing power is lodged in a single representative body—such as the British House of Commons or the Israeli Knesset. America has nothing like that because its framers did not trust the people enough. Their human ontology—a theory of what it means to be human—suggested this was a bad idea. The Constitution makes two assumptions about human beings that separate it from the simple republics of the modern world.

First, human virtue is too often in short supply. People are certainly capable of working tremendous good, but also horrifying evil. And more commonly, we simply put our everyday interests above those of our community. This selfishness is part of human nature and cannot be changed. If it is true of one person, then it is also true of many, which means that the rule of the majority can be dangerous. Government institutions must therefore stop self-interested majorities from enriching themselves at the expense of everybody else.

Second, the human ability to understand the world is limited. The faculty of reason is no doubt an amazing capacity, separating us from beasts, but it does not make us omniscient. And we have a bad habit of refusing to acknowledge the limits of what we know. This is especially true on matters of right and wrong. We tend to see what is good for us as being objectively good, even when it is not.

Let's look at both assumptions in a bit more detail, beginning with the problem of human morality. Are human beings naturally good? That question has been the source of controversy throughout Western political thought for centuries, often dividing the right from the left. Even the names "left" and "right" derive indirectly from that question, as the more radical members of the French Revolution, who believed that reason could perfect human morals, sat on the left-hand side of the National Assembly, while those who preferred the anchors of tradition sat on the right.

We can appreciate the competing ideas of left and right on human goodness by juxtaposing two men of the 18th century, Thomas Paine and David Hume, whose writings influenced the framers. Paine, the famous English-born polemicist who helped spur the American colonies to rebellion with the book *Common Sense*, was supremely confident that a novus homo was emerging in the Age of Enlightenment.[4] He argued in the *Rights of Man*,

> There is a morning of reason rising upon man on the subject
> of government, that has not appeared before. As the barbarism
> of the present old governments expires, the moral conditions of
> nations with respect to each other will be changed.[5]

This, Paine envisioned, would bring about a revolution in what it means to be human. "Man will not be brought up with the savage idea of considering his species as his enemy, because the accident of birth gave the individuals existence in countries distinguished by different names."[6] In other words, human goodness will flourish once the barbaric superstitions of the past are done away with.

Paine's ideas have proven remarkably durable. Woodrow Wilson, 28th president of the United States, gave a modern expression to Paine's argument in his pre-presidential writings. "A full century had gone by since the government of the nation was set up," he argued in the late 19th century.[7] Since then, the country had "drawn together to a common life." Communities that were once separated were now united; people had a better understanding of "the interests of society everywhere."[8] From Wilson's perspective, the America of 1887 was a markedly different nation than when the framers wrote the Constitution in 1787. Back then, the people may have been ignorant, factional, and unfit to rule except for indirectly. But 100 years later, Wilson saw a truly national people, animated by "the common consciousness, the common interests, the common standards of conduct, (and) the habit of concerted action."[9]

This is not the view of human nature on which the framers based the Constitution. While most framers certainly believed that the Enlightenment could improve morality by sweeping away past prejudices, they still saw an intrinsic selfishness in the human soul that could never truly be done away with. For this, they owed a debt to the Scottish philosopher David Hume, who not only rejected Paine's idea that reason can triumph over selfish passions but even went so far as to claim that "reason is and ought only to be the slave of the passions" and that it "can never pretend to any other office than to serve and obey them."[10] From Hume's perspective, reason is a natural tool wielded by man to satisfy his wants, just as a claw is for the tiger. The notion that reason can overcome those wants is self-contradictory. It is this "frailty and perverseness" of human nature, as Hume put it, that requires us to form government. We know that "justice" is necessary "to maintain peace and order," but we are "seduced . . . by the allurement of present, though often very frivolous temptations." This condition, Hume noted, "is incurable," and it is why government must exist.[11]

Hume was an atheist (and indeed many founders were either deists or unorthodox Protestants), but his moral theory had a corollary in the Reformed tradition of John Calvin, whose *Institutes of the Christian Religion* remains one of the most important books in Christian history.[12] Calvin believed that human beings were so thoroughly infested by original sin that their salvation depended entirely on God. Though the French-born Calvin taught in Geneva, his ideas formed the theological basis for the English and Scottish Reformations and thus were common in America. The Presbyterians, Anglicans, and Congregationalists were all Calvinist in some form or another. Many non-English speakers in the American colonies, like the Dutch and some segments of German immigrants, were Calvinist. Even if one was not a Christian, it was hard to get away from Calvin in America in the 1700s. Madison is a good example. He was never much of a religious man, but he was educated by Calvinist instructors, and his skepticism of natural human goodness reflected this background.

If the framers were dubious of human morality, they were likewise skeptical of our capacity to understand the world. Again, they believed that the Enlightenment's emphasis on science and reason had elucidated many mysteries of existence. But they still saw limits, especially when it came to circumstances when the interests of the individual conflict with the good of the whole community. The framers thought that people have a pernicious tendency to believe that what is good for them is good for all, even when it is not.

The complexity of the world is beyond what any one person, group of people, generation, or even civilization can comprehend. As such, traditional notions and systems should be preferred over untried and novel innovations—not necessarily a decisive advantage, but that the tried and true is usually preferable to the novel. Edmund Burke argued forcefully for this view in his defense of the British constitution against those who sought to do to Britain what the French Revolution did to France. In *Reflections on the Revolution in France*, he wrote,

> We are afraid to put men to live and trade each on his own private stock of reason; because we suspect that this stock in each man is small, and that the individuals would do better to avail themselves of the general bank and capital of nations and ages.[13]

A better summary of the limits of human understanding is hard to find: Individuals barely understand the world, but humanity over the centuries has nevertheless slowly created wise institutions.

In the 20th century, philosopher Karl Popper and economist F. A. Hayek forcefully restated Burke's insight. Popper believed that human knowledge was a product only of empirical trial and error and that seemingly established propositions must remain forever provisional. He acknowledged that

> we know a great deal, but our ignorance is sobering and boundless. With each step forward, with each problem which we solve, we not only discover new and unsolved problems, but we also discover that where we believed that we were standing on

firm and safe ground, all things are, in truth, insecure and in a
state of flux.[14]

Hayek, meanwhile, applied this notion of limits to man's efforts to reshape
society, arguing against the conceit of central planning. He asserted,
"It would be impossible for any mind to comprehend the infinite variety
of different needs of different people which compete for the available
resources and to attach a definite weight to each." The problem is the "limits of our powers of imagination," which render it impossible "to include
in our scale of values more than a sector of the needs of the whole society."[15] Popper and Hayek were not traditionalists. They both embraced an
open society and a market economy, in which ideas and goods are freely
exchanged. But just as Burke before them, they both opposed the assump-
tion that the world is easily comprehensible to the human mind.

While the framers predate Popper's, Hayek's, and Burke's forceful writings against radicalism, the Constitution nevertheless registers a skepticism about human understanding. Instead, the framers generally feared
that our view of the world is inevitably embroiled in what we want from
the world. In *Federalist* 10, Madison noted, "No man is allowed to be a judge
in his own cause; because his interest would certainly bias his judgment,
and, not improbably, corrupt his integrity."[16]

* * * *

These views were the general tendencies at the time of the founding. Not
all leaders of the era were equally skeptical of human goodness or understanding. Broadly speaking, there were three sets of views around 1787,
typified by the ideologies of Thomas Jefferson, Hamilton, and Madison.
Each used various threads of Enlightenment thought to weave a distinctively American political theory—specifically, about who should be the
dominant governing force in society. Madison's comes closest to embody-
ing the core ideology of the Constitution, but it is important to differenti-
ate him from Jefferson and Hamilton.

Jefferson, among the prominent men of the American founding, was
probably the closest to Paine, but notably he was in France at the time of the
Constitutional Convention, so he played no role in the deliberations. It is
too much to say that Jefferson was a democrat by contemporary standards,

but he had greater faith in humanity than most of his peers did—so long as two trends continued. The first was the promotion of education, to which Jefferson was profoundly committed. Education freed people from superstition and gave them a sense of how their fates were connected to those of the whole community. An educated people could thus be trusted to wield government power. This is why Jefferson spent his retirement founding the University of Virginia, one of the first public universities in the United States. The second was the proliferation of land ownership, which Jefferson believed promoted civic virtue. This idea harkened back to the Roman Republic, where the land-owning citizen was thought to be the backbone of free society. Such a man could feed himself and his family, liberating him from dependencies on the state or his fellows. This self-sufficiency made him an ideal citizen of a republic. Jefferson thought the yet-unsettled territories of America could create a nation of yeoman farmers fit to sustain the United States for generations to come.

Hamilton in contrast had great faith in a natural aristocracy. To be clear, he did not mean by this a title of nobility passed down as a patrimony from father to son, as was the case in the kingdoms of Europe. Rather, he believed there were those who, by virtue of natural endowment, possessed extraordinary qualities. Hamilton agreed with Hume that all men were governed by their passions, but he saw natural aristocrats as governed by nobler passions—ultimately, the desire to be remembered well by history. For Hamilton, the perfect embodiment of such a man was Washington. The task of republican government was to elevate these individuals to power, with the masses participating only indirectly in the affairs of state.

Hamilton's view was more popular among the northern delegates to the Constitutional Convention—Massachusetts, New York, and Pennsylvania. This is ironic in a sense because the South was more aristocratic in culture, yet it speaks to the increasing commercialization of the North. In cities such as Boston, Philadelphia, and New York City, there were opportunities for men of natural talents to build a fortune and a reputation. Those who accomplished this had demonstrated that they were set apart.

Many framers shared some aspects of Hamilton's view, although there were differences among them. Gouverneur Morris of Pennsylvania, for instance, favored giving the elites a privileged position in the Senate, but that was partly due to fear. He worried that the wealthy would take control of the whole government if they were not kept in check. John Adams, then serving as minister to Great Britain, was of a similar mind. And though Madison generally eschewed the elitism of Hamilton, he believed it had some merit. Advising those designing a state constitution for Kentucky in the 1780s, for instance, he suggested that property ownership be a qualification for holding the office of senator.

While Hamilton would be a central figure in the economic and foreign policy disputes of the Washington administration, his influence at the Constitutional Convention was limited. His views were too far out of step with most delegates, and he was absent from its proceedings for long stretches of time. If anything, the Constitution mainly reflects Madison's view of human nature. This is not to imply that Madison prevailed upon his fellow delegates to see human beings as he did, but rather his political writings better encapsulated the consensus of the delegates.

Like Jefferson, Madison believed that education and land ownership would certainly promote virtue, but he did not think they would go nearly as far. Like Hamilton, Madison believed in a natural aristocracy, but he was unwilling to hand over so much power to it. Instead, Madison trusted nobody to play the role of the "disinterested [and] dispassionate umpire," as he had written to Washington.[17] So what was to be done? Madison offered an ingenious alternative. Instead of empowering a certain group to serve as umpire, he would entrust it to the political process itself. The key, in Madison's view, was to ensure that no faction dominates the rest. Absent such a hegemon, no group can get everything it wants. To achieve the best deal possible, the various factions of society will have to negotiate with each other. As each angles for its own advantage, it blocks the most egregious demands of the others. Over time, something approaching a common interest emerges, as factions converge on a policy they can all live with.

Such a process would only be possible in a diverse polity. From Madison's perspective, Montesquieu had it exactly backward. Small republics are not sustainable because interests are so uniform that eventually a dominant faction would emerge to tyrannize the rest. So it had been with the 13 states under the Articles of Confederation. The commercial class in Boston was so dominant that it could rule all of Massachusetts. Likewise, the poor farmers of Rhode Island had nobody to thwart their most selfish demands. And religious intolerance had thrived for so long in Virginia because of the dominance of an Anglican majority. But if the United States were to become a true national republic, rather than a confederation of states, there could never be such a hegemon. Ultimately, the problem had been one of scale. A democratic republic could be a sustainable form of government, but it had to be practiced at a national level.

This idea formed the basis of the Virginia Plan, authored by Madison and submitted by the Virginia delegation at the Constitutional Convention in May 1787. In Madison's system, Congress would have virtually unlimited power, able to pass any law necessary for the national interest, and even veto state laws that thwart the public good. It would also represent the people of the United States, as both Madison's house and his senate would be based on proportional representation. His belief was that a truly national congress could be a reliable steward of such powers, because the diversity of the people would force it to compromise and ultimately adopt views that reflect a national consensus.

In some ways, Madison's ideas represent the pinnacle of Enlightenment thought, treating questions of justice and the general welfare not as matters of morality but rather as part of "the science of politics," as both Madison and Hamilton refer to it in the Federalist Papers.[18] Just as an engineer builds a machine to redirect the natural forces of the world for useful ends, so Madison's plan of government would rechannel human selfishness toward the general good. But there is more going on here than a simple balancing and countering of selfish forces. Politics for Madison was also a process of discovery. It induces human beings to collectively overcome their personal limits, to begin to appreciate how the interests of one can be harmonized with those of others. Individuals enter political community with a purely selfish understanding of their interests, but through it, they participate in the triumph of the common good. Madison was never inclined to the Aristotelian view that politics helps us become truly human, but his theory does imply that it can help us broaden our perspectives, to see how our own interests are inevitably bound up with those of our neighbors.

In such a system, democratic legitimacy is a necessary condition of public action. The rich or wellborn do not occupy a privileged position, but instead count as one faction among many. Determinations about public action must be made by the people at large. But the rules of the game are set up to prevent majority factions from dominating the system. Instead, governing majorities should be larger and broader than half plus one, bringing a multitude of factions into the coalition. They also need to be considered and durable, based on extensive conversations and give-and-take between the different groups in society. Such majorities are more likely to reflect the true public interest.

In a sense, Madison was making an empirical wager—never stated explicitly, but made nonetheless. He knew that degeneration into mob rule was the chief danger of a democratic republic; some faction that amounts to a majority seizes power for its own sake, rather than the good of all citizens. But he believed that the probability of this happening decreased when the majority's position reflected a consensus view of society. It was no guarantee, of course, but it was more likely than not.

One can appreciate this idea by imagining two hypothetical majorities. One constitutes two-thirds of both chambers of Congress and emerges after a robust and extensive political debate. The other is a flash-in-the-pan majority in the House that barely makes it to the minimum of 218 votes. Without knowing anything about the policy debate going on, which is more likely to be in the public interest? The former, obviously. No doubt, that will not always be the correct guess. Sometimes the former opinion will be unjust. Sometimes a narrow majority will have understood the best interest of the community. But over time, the smart bet is that the large, broad, and considered majority is benevolent while the small, narrow, and fleeting one is not.

These ideas are "Madisonian" in the sense that Madison articulated them more ably than any of his contemporaries did. Yet while he certainly was influential in pointing his fellow framers in this direction, he did not have to do a lot of prodding. Most of them were stuck, like Madison, somewhere between Hamilton and Jefferson, doubting the goodness of the masses and the elites. Most of them believed that institutions could be designed according to Enlightenment principles of politics to redirect selfish impulses toward the benefit of the community. This doctrine of consensus was appealing to them.

Indeed, they modeled this principle in Philadelphia. While matters at the Constitutional Convention were decided by a plurality of states present, issues could always be revisited, and there was an expectation that, on balance, every faction among them should walk away with something. Likewise, the Constitution became law only when nine of 13 states, or better than a two-thirds majority, ratified it after an extensive debate— the very essence of consensus. The story of the Constitution is one of compromise after compromise, to build the largest, broadest, and most considered coalition in favor of ratification.

That is what the Constitution imposes on the national government. The result is a lawmaking process in which the full diversity of the United States may be reflected. In such a national republic, the expectation is that social, economic, or political factions will struggle to dominate the rest.

3

Checks and Balances

As 18th-century republicans, the framers were committed to the doctrine of popular sovereignty. They believed that the only legitimate source of power was the people and that all leaders must be accountable in some way to them. But as skeptics of human goodness and understanding, they also expected that the people sometimes would make bad choices. They were particularly anxious about selfish majorities, which in a simple democratic process can seize the power of the government for their own ends. They resolved this tension by embracing the doctrine of consensus, as argued in Chapter 2. The people would be sovereign, but the national republic would empower majorities that were larger, broader, and more considered, as these were most likely to reflect the true interests of the community.

This sort of republic would have to be representative, in which the people exercise power through elected officials. This necessitates some group of political elites, who rule on the people's behalf. The framers thought this would help the republic. By virtue of their education, public preeminence, wealth, or intelligence, they can "refine and enlarge the public views," as James Madison put it in *Federalist* 10.[1] In this way, representation helps consensus by making public majorities more deliberative.

Of course, elites are human, prone to the same selfish tendencies that can undermine popular sovereignty. How to keep them in line? The framers agreed with Montesquieu that the government's legislative, executive, and judicial functions had to be separated. Centralizing all power in one place would enable some elites to gain too much control and thus was a path to tyranny. But it was one thing to declare those powers separated; it was quite another to keep them that way. What was to stop some willful and ambitious leader from conniving to collect the powers that a constitution had separated? To address this problem, the framers turned to the history of the Roman Republic, especially how it used power sharing to keep elites in check. The framers would reshape Roman ideas, mixing them with ideas borrowed from Montesquieu, into what we today call checks and balances.

Checks and balances are thus another way of building consensus. Just as no faction in the country can dominate the rest, so, too, can no group of elites dominate others. Nobody holds the preponderance of power, either in the public or in the halls of government. Just as different popular factions must bargain with each other, the only way for elites to achieve their political goals is to compromise.

* * * *

In today's era of populist fervor, "elites" might as well be a four-letter word. People on the left and the right believe that our politics has been hijacked by the elites, who have been bribed by the ultrarich to tilt public policy toward their own ends. The best way to reform the government is to put the people in charge, or so the thinking goes.

The framers had a different perspective. The Constitution essentially establishes a group of political elites through the process of representation. The people themselves do not make policy decisions, but rather elect representatives to make those decisions on their behalf. These professional politicians make up the core of our system's elites and were supplemented early on by high-level officials in the executive branches, like the secretaries of Treasury and state.

There was no way to establish a national republic by any other means. Even in 1787, the country was far too large for direct democracy. From the framers' point of view, representative democracy was not simply a necessity, but a virtue. If the national republic promotes large and broad majorities, representation promotes deliberative ones. The process of election would, as Madison wrote in *Federalist* 10,

> enlarge the public views, by passing them through the medium of a chosen body of citizens, whose wisdom may best discern the true interest of their country, and whose patriotism and love of justice, will be least likely to sacrifice it to temporary or partial considerations.[2]

In other words, the hope was that while the people are not capable of judging every issue with wisdom and dispassion, they can at least identify among themselves those individuals of special character who can. This is what the framers thought of as the "natural aristocracy"—not one based on inherited titles, but on the possession of certain, noble traits that made some people uniquely fit for service to the community. Granted, America has had more than its fair share of disreputable politicians, but it has also had many individuals who were, to borrow the title of John F. Kennedy's Pulitzer Prize–winning book, *Profiles in Courage*.[3]

The virtues of representation would have their fullest expression in the Senate. With their longer terms of office and appointment by the state legislatures, senators would, as John Dickinson said, be "distinguished for their rank in life and their weight of property, and bearing as strong a likeness to the British House of Lords as possible."[4] Madison hoped that the Senate would provide stability for the new government, thanks to senators' greater "acquaintance with the objects and principles of legislation." He expected that House members would get called from "pursuits of a private nature" to serve and would eventually be forced to return. They would not have enough time to do a thorough "study of the laws, the affairs and the comprehensive interests of their country." But senators, with six-year terms, would have that opportunity. They would likewise facilitate stability in Congress, as the House could see "a rapid succession of new members," which could conceivably lead to a frequent "change of measures," which is "inconsistent with every rule of prudence."[5]

Over the subsequent centuries, scholars of politics have put forward several models of representation that help clarify how it gives public laws a deliberateness they might otherwise lack. One framework is often called the delegate model, which holds that a representative acts mainly as a cipher for the public views. His role is to overcome the sheer impracticality of direct democracy. It is impossible for all the people of his district to be present at the seat of government, so he is there to act as they would. Many opponents of the Constitution preferred this model, and as such, they favored procedures like annual elections, instructed voting (requiring members to vote according to the will of the community), and recall petitions. All of this was meant to tether the representative to the community's opinions as tightly as possible.

But most advocates of the Constitution supported greater leeway for legislators to make up their own minds. That points to a second style of representation, often called the trustee model. This holds that the task of the representative is to reflect the best interests of his constituents, which means that he must follow his own conscience. The benefits of trustee-ship found a forceful defense from British theorist and politician Edmund Burke, who in a letter to his constituents wished to be "in the strictest union, the closest correspondence, and the most unreserved communication with his constituents." But that could not always be the case. While the representative should give "great weight" to their views and "unre-mitted attention" to "their business," he must never sacrifice "his unbi-assed opinion, his mature judgment," or "his enlightened conscience." For he owes the representative "his judgment," which must never be "sacri-fice[d]" to the opinions of his constituents, unless they can persuade him they are correct.[6]

The third type of representation is a mix of the two and is sometimes called the politico model. The idea is that as a matter of everyday politics, representatives pick and choose between the delegate and trustee model. On issues in which voter interest is low and public opinions are unformed, representatives act as trustees, doing what they think is best for their community. (Or at least the good ones will; there are always corrupt or ignorant politicians who sacrifice their constituents' interests for their own ambitions, venality, or wealth.) But on matters in which voters are deeply engaged and have strong opinions, representatives will act as dele-gates, lest they face the wrath of the public at the next election for voting against their constituents.

Practically speaking, the politico model makes the most sense. It maximizes politicians' freedom to make their own judgments while min-imizing the risk of electoral backlash. And the politico model is good for the community, too, as it promotes consensus. For the public to get what it wants, its views must be considered. Inchoate public impulses are less likely to influence outcomes in Congress than strong demands are, since members know they can vote their own preferences with the for-mer but not with the latter. This gives greater leeway to representatives to fashion compromises with each other for their constituents' mutual interests. Then again, public passions are more likely to come into play when they are strongly felt, which in turn suggests issues that the people have thought more deeply about. In those circumstances, members of Congress are more likely to defer.

* * * *

Of course, political elites are also a potential problem for free government. While the United States in the 1780s had witnessed the dangers of excessive democracy, most of world history is a story of political elites attacking the people's liberties or sacrificing their safety to slake their own ambitions—for glory, conquest, and treasure. Indeed, in the Europe from which Americans had emigrated, the overwhelming majority of people had toiled for the benefit of a few. The framers knew well the potential trouble elites could cause. After all, they were human beings— full of selfish impulses that drove them to place the good of themselves first. Something had to be done about them, just as something had to be done about the public at large.

Montesquieu had advised separating the powers of government, so that no single elite or faction could gain total control. The framers certainly agreed with the great French philosopher but did not think he went far enough. He had argued that in theory the British constitution separated powers, but the Americans believed that the division was actually fictitious. The legislative power theoretically belonged to Parliament, but practically speaking, the king's ministers used royal patronage to secure the legislation they preferred. In searching beyond the example of Great Britain, the Americans found important lessons in the history of the Roman Republic.

Rome loomed large in the American imagination. George Washington modeled himself on Cincinnatus, the Roman general who, according to legend, took command when the republic was in danger but gave it up when peace had been secured. Alexander Hamilton and Madison used the pseudonym "Publius" for the Federalist Papers, in honor of Publius Valerius Publicola, who helped overthrow the Etruscan monarchy that preceded the republic. The US Capitol is named after the Capitoline Hill in Rome, and the Capitol building borrows heavily from Roman architecture, as do many buildings in Washington, DC. And of course, the Senate was named after the Roman Senate.

According to tradition, the Romans overthrew their king in 506 BC. In fits and starts over the next 300 years, their system of government evolved into the republic that Polybius would document in his *Histories*, written in the 2nd century BC.[7] Polybius praised the Roman system for blending the rule of the one (through the consulship), the few (the Senate), and the many (the assembly), thus creating a government in which the defects of each type could be countered by that of the others.

No doubt, Polybius's account was highly stylized. There were, after all, two consuls and a multitude of lower elected officials with their own executive power. So there was really no rule of "the one." And while any Roman citizen had the right to vote in the assembly, the system privileged wealthier, older, and urban citizens. It was hardly the rule of "the many." Yet even if Polybius strained to make the Roman Republic fit his theory, he still understood that the genius of the Roman system lay in its elaborate network of power sharing among the elites. This prevented the Roman Republic's degeneration into tyranny, for when any elite or group of elites tried to seize power for themselves, they were met with a swift response from other elites. By granting multiple groups a share of power, rather than all of it, the Romans encouraged their elites to direct their ambitions, vanities, and desires toward the glory of the state.

For the elite Roman citizen, *dignitas* was the measure of your identity. It was a kind of informal credit system in the upper echelon of Roman society, delineating how much weight one carried in the eyes of one's fellow citizens. The best way to earn *dignitas* was through victory on the battlefield. Another way was to follow what the Romans called the cursus honorum, or the traditional sequence of offices held by rising elites. One would start with election to a minor office like the quaestorship, which oversaw the Roman treasury. Other offices would follow—aedile (managing public works), praetor (managing the judiciary), and finally the consul, which controlled the armies and generally was considered the leader of the Roman state.

The Romans elected multiple men to each office every year. The more minor offices could have more than 20, while the consulship was limited to two. Most offices were restricted to a 12-month term, and until late in the Roman Republic, it was not possible to stand for the same office twice in a row. Thus, many elite Romans could wield a share of power, if only for a time. Those men who passed through the upper ranks of the cursus honorum could enjoy a kind of semiretirement in the Roman Senate. The Roman Senate's formal powers were relatively limited, but it exercised vast discretion in both domestic and foreign affairs, because it contained within it the collected wisdom of the Roman elite.

It was a remarkable accomplishment. The Romans took all the selfish passions that usually brought down a good state and transformed them into the foundation of the republic. Rather than concentrating power in the hands of a few, the Romans spread it around, with no officeholder able to dominate the others. And because the offices were elected by the citizenry in the assemblies, Roman elites had an incentive to do a good job, lest their rise through the cursus honorum be halted.

But of course, the Roman Republic came to an end in the 1st century BC. After Julius Caesar declared himself dictator for life, old-guard republicans in the Senate assassinated him, plunging the republic into a civil war. After the Battle of Actium in 31 BC, his grandnephew, Octavian, stood triumphant, having vanquished all the contenders for preeminence. While he retained the forms of the republic, he effectively centralized all power around himself. By the time Octavian's heirs had all died, the Romans never thought of returning to a republic. It was now an empire.

Many writers over the centuries have explained the collapse of the republic as a product of declining civic virtue. Maybe so, but by the 1st century BC, the Roman Republic had constitutional problems as well. The power-sharing system had begun to break down. For most of its history, the Republic relied on unpaid armies of citizen-farmers who sacrificed their own interests to protect the community. But a series of massive wars, including the conflicts against Carthage in the Punic Wars (264–146 BC), the conquest of Greece by 146 BC, and Pompey the Great's conquest of the eastern Mediterranean in the 1st century BC, had obviated the old system. After these triumphs, the Roman army was highly professionalized and expected to be paid. But it was not the Roman Senate that saw to its payment; it was the generals, who paid it in plunder. The army switched its loyalty to the generals—Marius, Sulla, Pompey, and ultimately Caesar.

The American founders knew the Roman Republic's story well—the good and the bad. It had been drilled into them since they were boys. Madison's education is illustrative. As the son of the wealthiest planter in Orange County, Virginia, Madison had enjoyed private tutors, who emphasized a humanist education. As such, he was taught Latin and Greek and read authors such as Plutarch, Polybius, and Tacitus. As revolutionary fervor was picking up steam in the 1770s, Madison's reading of the republican era in Rome took on stronger resonance—for here was a people that had overthrown their king and established a system of government that lasted for centuries thereafter. Granted, few men of the era had an education comparable to Madison, and only a handful rivaled his intelligence. Still, the stories of the Roman Republic were a kind of lingua franca during the period, a common reference point from which they would draw.

The framers combined Montesquieu's idea of the separation of powers with this Roman notion of power sharing. The legislative, executive, and judicial branches control most of their respective powers, but at the margins, the authority is blended. That way, as Madison put it, "all business liable to abuses" would "pass through separate hands, the one being a check on the other."[8] And especially sensitive to the abuse that could occur with war-making power, the framers were careful to divide it between the president and Congress—with the former commanding the army but the latter responsible for its organization and above all its funding. It was in this way that they addressed a major flaw of the Roman Republic. There would be no warlord who could use the ambiguities of the US Constitution to bring the whole system down.

It is remarkable how little disagreement there was at the Constitutional Convention over the principle of checks and balances, as it has come to be called. The delegates had heated battles over major issues such as slavery and the role of the state governments, but the general idea of power sharing within the government was never a major question. For instance, when Madison suggested that a way of preventing "those charged with the public happiness" from "betray[ing] their trust" was to "divide the trust between different bodies of men, who might watch [and] check each other," everybody in the room understood exactly what he met. This was a reference to the mighty Roman Republic and worthy of emulation by the Americans.[9]

The separation of powers met with more opposition once the Constitution was released to the public for consideration. The Anti-Federalists particularly hated the Senate. The framers made the upper chamber the nexus for power sharing, among the legislative, executive, and judicial branches, for the Senate had a share in all of them. Anti-Federalists charged that this violated Montesquieu's maxim that power must be kept separate. As the pseudonymous Brutus wrote, "A separation of these powers should be sought as far as is practicable. I can scarcely imagine that any of the advocates of the system will pretend, that it was necessary to accumulate all these powers in the senate."[10]

In the Federalist Papers, the defense of checks and balances mainly fell to Madison, who developed his argument from *Federalist* 47 through *Federalist* 51. In *Federalist* 47, he followed Montesquieu in acknowledging that the "accumulation of all powers legislative, executive and judiciary . . . may justly be pronounced the very definition of tyranny." However, it was all right for a branch to have a "partial agency" in the affairs of another. So long as the "*whole* power of one department" is not exercised "by the same hands which possess the whole power of another department," power was still sufficiently separated.[11] (Emphasis in original.)

This, Madison asserted, was preferable to what he called in *Federalist* 48 "parchment barriers," or a mere declaration that the branches were to be separate. These might "mark with precision" the divisions between the branches but would not hold up "against the encroaching spirit of power," especially the "legislative department," which thanks to its "extensive" constitutional powers can with "greater facility" encroach "on the co-ordinate departments."[12] In *Federalist* 49, Madison likewise rejected the recourse of frequent constitutional conventions to correct violations, because—among other reasons—such "experiments are of too ticklish a nature to be unnecessarily multiplied," for as interest "too strongly the public passions."[13]

This paved the way for Madison's explanation of checks and balances in *Federalist* 51, an essay of such incredible importance it deserves to be quoted at length:

> In order to lay a due foundation for that separate and distinct exercise of the different powers of government, which to a certain extent, is admitted on all hands to be essential to the preservation of liberty, it is evident that each department should have a will of its own; and consequently should be so constituted, that the members of each should have as

little agency as possible in the appointment of the members of the others. . . .

It is equally evident that the members of each department should be as little dependent as possible on those of the others, for the emoluments annexed to their offices. Were the executive magistrate, or the judges, not independent of the legislature in this particular, their independence in every other would be merely nominal.[14]

The financial security of government officers is an important aspect of our system of government, although it is easy for us to take it for granted today. Salaries are set by law, and Congress is not allowed to diminish the president's or judges' pay. Likewise, the president is unable to offer government patronage to members of Congress. That keeps each branch from influencing the personal interests of the members of the others.

Yet salaries are just the start. Madison goes on:

But the great security against a gradual concentration of the several powers in the same department, consists in giving to those who administer each department, the necessary constitutional means, and personal motives, to resist encroachments of the others. The provision for defence must in this, as in all other cases, be made commensurate to the danger of attack. Ambition must be made to counteract ambition. The interest of the man must be connected with the constitutional rights of the place. . . .

A dependence on the people is no doubt the primary controul on the government; but experience has taught mankind the necessity of auxiliary precautions.

This policy of supplying by opposite and rival interests, the defect of better motives, might be traced through the whole system of human affairs, private as well as public.[15]

Madison offered two crucial ideas here. First, each distinct part of the government should have an independent political will. Neither the Senate, nor the House, nor the president can select members of the other. The states were to choose the senators, the people were to choose the House, and the Electoral College was to choose the president. Second, they should not be isolated from each other. Each must have the power to stop encroachments by the other. The House and Senate can reject the efforts of the other. The president can veto laws enacted by both chambers. Both chambers can override a veto and even remove a president. The underlying idea here is that because each of the three is chosen differently, its members will have their own selfish interests, which they will have the power to defend against assaults from the others. Without any clear force dominating the rest, the elites will ultimately have to share power with one another.

Madison's analysis in the above passage has a striking overlap with that laid out by Polybius in his *Histories*. Polybius argued that the Roman system kept the consuls, the assembly, and the Senate in check because,

> when any one of the three classes becomes puffed up, and manifests an inclination to be contentious and unduly encroaching, the mutual interdependency of all the three, and the possibility of the pretensions of any one being checked and thwarted by the others, must plainly check this tendency: and so the proper equilibrium is maintained by the impulsiveness of the one part being checked by its fear of the other.[16]

One can imagine Madison having his copy of the *Histories* opened to this page when writing *Federalist* 51.

Ultimately, the American system of checks and balances regulates political conflict, not just by creating rules for separated powers on a piece of "parchment," as Madison might say, but by giving elites the ability to enforce those rules against each other.[17] Thus, ambitious political officeholders who crave *dignitas* will ultimately have to work with one another to find common ground. In other words, they will have to reach a consensus with one another, which increases the chances that what they do is for the benefit of the people, rather than for themselves.

In this way, checks and balances is an analogue to the national republic. Both make sure that no faction can dominate the other—be they in the country at large or the halls of power. The framers did not depend on elites or common people to always be selfless and virtuous. They instead expected everybody to often act selfishly, so they designed the rules of our political system to make sure that selfish motives counteract selfish motives. The rules of the political game, for both elites and the mass public, were intended to encourage compromise around broadly acceptable solutions that reflect the consensus of the body politic.

4

The Lawmaking Process

Congress is the most important governing institution in our nation, a claim that might come as a bit of a surprise. It is common nowadays to think our government is one of coequal branches. Even members of Congress say this. A few years ago, I took a group of high school students on a tour of the Capitol, and the introductory video *produced for Congress* declared Congress was a coequal branch. I couldn't believe it. The truth is that while the branches of our government are coordinate, in that they wield a unique type of government power, they are not coequal. Rather, Congress is at the heart of American government.

The people in our nation are bound by laws that they themselves have a role in writing. That only happens through Congress. The main duty of the executive is to enforce the laws created by the people's representatives in Congress, and the court's task is to resolve disputes arising under laws made by Congress. Both branches are of course important, but Congress is where Lincoln's immortal definition of republicanism—"government of the people, by the people, for the people"[1]—actually takes on real meaning. Indeed, while the Constitution establishes the president and the Supreme Court, it leaves much of the specific organization of the executive and judicial branches to laws written by Congress. On the other hand, each chamber of Congress has exclusive authority over its own rules and the sole power to punish and remove its members.

The inherent power of Congress carries with it a danger that points back to the essential problem of government. If the people, and by extension their representatives, are the sovereign lawmaking authority, what happens if they misrule? What if the people want something that is bad for the community? What if their representatives undermine the public interest for their own glory? There is no king to check these excesses. There is no aristocratic nobility to create balance within the body politic or the legislative assembly. Having wholeheartedly embraced the idea of a democratic republic, the framers had to find a way to make it behave itself. The solution to this problem was the idea of consensus. The larger, broader, and more considered coalition in favor of a proposal, the more likely it reflects the true community interests.

While Chapters 2 and 3 discussed these ideas theoretically, this chapter examines how the lawmaking process implements them practically. The Constitution establishes the rules of the system so both the mass public and political elites are more likely to achieve consensus.

The Constitution encourages consensus among lawmakers in three important ways. First, the House of Representatives, by representing the people of the nation directly, takes in all the diversity of our continental republic. That makes it difficult for a single faction to dominate, which in turn forces a process of bargaining to find a solution that satisfies multiple groups. Second, there is the unique role of the Senate. Population does not matter in the Senate; instead, every state has two votes regardless of its inhabitants. This protects geographically distinct minorities, which might not be sufficiently represented in the House, from having their interests overrun by factions that are concentrated in some places but not others. Then, as a final, independent check on Congress, the framers invested the president with the power of the veto to make sure that the law reflects the national interest.

* * * *

The place to start with Congress is the organization of popular sovereignty, for that is where it differs so markedly from other democratic institutions throughout the world. Congress is not designed to empower a simple majority, but rather to reflect a wide array of views. This idea is most evident in James Madison's *Federalist* 10, arguably his most important contribution to all the Federalist Papers. In it, Madison asserted that a large democratic republic is better than a small one. The key for Americans was to "extend the sphere" of republican government beyond the states, embracing a truly national union.[2]

To develop this idea, Madison leaned on David Hume and other skeptics of intrinsic human goodness. Madison argued that the spirit of factionalism—or the tendency to put ourselves and those like us above the interests of all—is "sown into the nature of man," so much so that we "see [it] everywhere." The "most common and durable source of factions" is economic, specifically, "the various and unequal distributions of property." Madison saw such conflicts coming from multiple angles: those with property and those without, creditors and debtors, and the different interests among farmers, merchants, bankers, workers, and others.[3]

"The principal task of modern legislation," Madison argued, is to regulate these competing interests.[4] But that is easier said than done. The problem, as he had told George Washington privately in the spring of 1787, is that there is no "dispassionate umpire" to arbitrate these kinds of disputes.[5] In *Federalist* 10, Madison noted that in a simple democracy, strength of numbers matters more than fairness. The victor in a factional dispute will typically be "the most numerous party," regardless of the justice of its claims. In conflicts between farmers and merchants, creditors and debtors, and capital owners and laborers, the standard of justice too often is might makes right.[6]

Montesquieu held that a small, virtue-loving republic of uniform interests would minimize this sort of conflict. But Madison believed the experience of the American states had contradicted this. Instead, a small society was less likely to sustain a republic because it was more likely to have a hegemonic faction:

> The smaller the society, the fewer probably will be the distinct parties and interests composing it; the fewer the distinct parties and interests, the more frequently will a majority be found of the same party; and the smaller the number of individuals composing a majority, and the smaller the compass within which they are placed, the more easily will they concert and execute their plans of oppression.[7]

On the other hand, a larger society would be more diverse and less likely to have a dominant faction, a situation that would be good for republican government:

> Extend the sphere, and you take in a greater variety of parties and interests; you make it less probable that a majority of the whole will have a common motive to invade the rights of other citizens; or if such a common motive exists, it will be more

difficult for all who feel it to discover their own strength, and to act in unison with each other.[8]

What would such a polity look like? What happens in a diverse state where there is no dominant interest group? The answer is that the various forces in society will have to bargain with one another. Nobody gets everything they want. Everybody must compromise. The proposal that can pass muster in a diverse polity, after such extensive negotiations, is more likely to be in the interests of the whole community.

Madison believed that no single person or group can serve as the dispassionate umpire to resolve political, social, and economic disputes. Nobody can possibly be above the fray, for human beings are too self-interested by nature. But that does not matter. In a diverse polity with many different interests, the political process can empower factions to police each other. The selfish demands of one group will be countered by the demands of another group, whose demands will likewise be countered, and so on, until a proposal is identified that can meet with widespread approval. This, of course, is no guarantee: The essential problem of government is just that— essential, built into the very nature of humanity. Madison understood this and argued that a diverse republic creates only a "tendency to break and control the violence of faction."[9] So unjust laws could still be enacted, and fair laws could be voted down. But this "extended" republic, as Madison called it, is better than any alternative yet devised.

This logic underpins the House of Representatives, whose members are distributed among the states according to the population of each. The framers intended it to represent the people of the United States of America, rather than the individual states. The belief was that the House would reflect the diversity of the people and so could never be dominated by a single faction.

Madison's arguments seem to be in line with the contemporary idea that democracy is a good thing. But that is not exactly what he was asserting. Rather, he was trying to prevent democracy from destroying the republic. He thought democracy was necessary for a republic but not sufficient. The people must be the ultimate rulers in a republic, but steps must be taken to keep them from abusing that power. The real agenda behind *Federalist* 10 is finding a way to make democracy work without needing a king or aristocratic class. Madison's alternative was the careful distribution of political power in a large, diverse republic.

* * * *

If the House of Representatives makes sense according to contemporary democratic theory, the Senate seems downright baffling. Many Americans today are left wondering how it is fair for the states to be equal in the upper chamber. Why should Wyoming have the same number of senators as California does? The Senate seems more like a vestigial organ from a time before people were as committed to democracy as we are today. Yet the Senate does make sense when we think about our government in terms of consensus. We must do a little digging into the historical record to appreciate it, but the logic is there.

There was widespread agreement at the Constitutional Convention that Congress should be divided into two chambers. Bicameralism, as this is known, was necessary to control both popular factions in society at large and to keep elites from overrunning popular government for their own ends. Roger Sherman of Connecticut spoke for the delegates when he said that the legislature was "the depository of the supreme will of society," but most of them were worried about Congress becoming too powerful.[10] In a republic, the legislature, as the collective embodiment of the will of the people, has a tendency "to throw all power into" its "vortex," as Madison put it.[11] That could undermine the independence of the executive branch and the judiciary. One way to keep the legislature in line was to split it into two halves, each with a power base independent of the other. Not everybody agreed with this—Benjamin Franklin being a notable advocate of a single chamber of Congress—but most of them advocated two chambers of Congress.

Bicameralism helps promote consensus by regulating public opinion. The people rule Congress, but by separating it into two chambers, the framers gave the legislature a kind of split personality. The two halves must agree before a bill becomes a law. A narrow or intemperate majority in the House can be checked by a more reasonable one in the Senate, or vice versa. The framers likewise thought that the Senate—with its longer terms and indirect elections by state legislatures—would be somewhat removed from the people, thus bringing a degree of stability and wisdom to government deliberations. The House would reflect the momentary changes in public opinion, but the Senate would be better able to capture the underlying currents of the body politic.

Bicameralism additionally limits the potential havoc that elites can play against the public good. As Madison argued in *Federalist* 62, it "doubles the security to the people, by requiring the concurrence of two distinct bodies in schemes of usurpation or perfidy, where the ambition or corruption of one, would otherwise be sufficient."[12]

Nevertheless, if there is one part of the United States Constitution that does not conform to Madison's plan of government, it is the United States Senate. Madison wanted *a* senate, of course, as it would hopefully be a repository of policy expertise, civic virtue, and moderate passions. But he did not want *the* Senate as it is in the Constitution. Instead, he preferred the upper chamber to be apportioned like the House, according to population. He thought that if the logic of the extended republic was going to work, it had to apply to both chambers. If the Senate were apportioned equally, then it would not reflect the multifaceted interests of the whole people, but the majority factions in each state. The narrowness of state polities, in Madison's view, had brought the country to crisis under the Articles of Confederation, and it made no sense to him to import this defect into the new government.

So why did the Constitutional Convention reject Madison's proposal for a population-based senate? Unfortunately, the Federalist Papers, which typically reflect the delegates' opinions, do not really answer the question, perhaps because both Hamilton and Madison hated the design of the Senate. Madison touched on the Senate's equal representation in *Federalist* 62, but it was little more than a grudging acknowledgment of the political necessities that led to a compromise. Compare that to his elaborate detailing of the national republic in *Federalist* 10, and one is left with the sense that there must have been more going on behind the scenes. To appreciate the logic of equal apportionment in the Senate, it is necessary to look a little more closely at the debates on the subject at the Constitutional Convention.

Madison's idea of a proportional senate held sway with a majority of delegates from six states—Massachusetts, Pennsylvania, Virginia, North Carolina, South Carolina, and Georgia. The first four of these were the most populous states, and while Georgia was small in terms of its population, it had vast territory and expected to be populous one day. Delegates from the small states—Connecticut, New Jersey, Delaware, and Maryland— disagreed and were joined by New York. Hamilton was a member of the New York delegation, but he was outvoted by John Lansing and Robert Yates, who wanted to retain as much sovereignty for their home state as possible. The small-state faction generally accepted the idea of proportional representation in the House of Representatives and instead made its play for the Senate, where it demanded equal apportionment.

The large states had a six-to-five advantage on the issue. But this was hardly an overwhelming edge, for it was based on the temporary absence of the New Hampshire delegates, who did not arrive until after the matter was resolved. Just as important, the small states were a vehement minority. They did not let the matter lie, even after the large states prevailed in a preliminary vote on the issue. Indeed, Delaware was so serious about equality of representation that the commission to its delegates explicitly "prohibited" them from "changing . . . the equality of votes among the states."[13]

The small states worried that proportional representation in both chambers would threaten the interests of their political communities. If the new government were premised entirely on a national majority, the people of the small states would constantly be under threat. Gunning Bedford Jr. of Delaware thought there were different interests among the states, particularly "rivalship of commerce, of manufactures," which had to be preserved.[14] Sherman of Connecticut agreed that the states had their own interests, so he thought it necessary that they be "equally and effectually guarded in society."[15]

From the perspective of the small states, a purely proportional system of government would lead inevitably to a democratic tyranny. William Paterson of New Jersey analogized Madison's plan for a proportional senate to the idea of giving the colonies a vote in the House of Commons before the Revolutionary War. "America," he said, "could not have been entitled to more than one-third of the number of representatives" in the British Parliament. "Would American rights and interests have been safe under an authority thus constituted?" No, he responded. So it was for New Jersey. "She would be swallowed up," and Paterson preferred to "submit to a monarch, to a despot" than the rule of a large-state majority.[16] Bedford likewise predicted that the "large states" would "crush the small ones whenever they stand in the way of their ambitions or interested views." Luther Martin of Maryland pledged he would never agree to a plan that "lay 10 states at the mercy of Virginia, Massachusetts, and Pennsylvania."[17]

The delegates from the large states had three major responses. First, they emphasized the injustice of minority rule. From Madison's perspective, an "equality of suffrage" between the states made sense under the Articles of Confederation but would not in the new government. The Articles of Confederation did not govern citizens directly. Instead, they amounted to a compact among the 13 states, which retained all the powers over the people.[18] So if Virginia thought the Continental Congress had enacted an unfair law, it could simply not enforce it. Under a national system, with the new government passing laws that taxed or regulated the people, it would be possible for a majority of states, representing a minority of the people, to rule the rest. As Madison put it, such a scheme "contradicts the fundamental maxim of republican government, which requires that the sense of the majority should prevail."[19] The small states found this unpersuasive, because they were already admitting proportionality in the House. They responded that there was no way for Delaware to rule Virginia. For them, the fear was Virginia ruling Delaware.

Second, the large-state delegates argued that the stubbornness of the small states was going to scuttle the Constitutional Convention and destroy the Union, at which point the small states would be in real danger. Madison noted that if "the union of the states be dissolved," then either the "small states" would be subject to the whims of the "ambition and power of their larger neighbors" or they would have to cut a deal with the big states, which would presumably "exact . . . concessions" much worse than what were proposed in the Virginia Plan.[20] Unsurprisingly, this argument did not go over well with the small-state delegates, who chafed at the thinly veiled threat of future doom. At one point, Bedford shocked many delegates when he predicted that the small states would ally with European powers, "who would take them by the hand and do them justice."[21]

The third and most persuasive rejoinder from the large-state delegates was that the republican theory of politics, whereby distinct interests must be protected from democratic overreach, simply did not apply to the small states. They were "imaginary beings," in the words of Wilson, not worthy of such protection.[22] Rufus King of Massachusetts argued that the goal of the Constitutional Convention was to "secure every *man* in America . . . all his rights" and not "sacrifice this substantial good to the phantom of *state* sovereignty."[23] (Emphasis in original.) Madison admitted that "wherever there is danger of attack there ought be given a constitutional power of defense."[24] But there was no danger to the small states from the large ones, for "too much stress was laid on the rank of the states as political societies. There was a gradation," with some communities possessing distinct interests and others not.[25] The states did not have distinct interests. In Madison's judgment, the relationship between the states and the national government was "parallel" to "the people of the townships" to the "states," undeserving of unique protections in government.[26]

Likewise, the large-state delegates did not see any common interests that could bring Massachusetts, Pennsylvania, and Virginia together. The differences among these states were just too great to overcome. And the larger the state, the more likely there would be significant rivalries within it. The most probable result would be ever-shifting alliances between small states and factions within large states.

Insofar as the states would become rivals, the large-state delegates did not think disputes would have anything to do with their size. Hamilton argued that the "only considerable distinction of interests lay between the carrying and non-carrying states"—that is, commercial and agricultural interests—"which divide instead of unit[e] the largest [s]tates."[27] Madison, anticipating future sectional troubles, argued that "the great division of interests in the United States . . . did not lie between the large and small states," but rather "between the northern and southern states," thanks in no small part to the institution of slavery. Again, the large states were divided on this issue.[28]

Perhaps the most fascinating feature of this debate is what both sides agreed on. They generally believed that a republic must protect individual rights and advance the good of all. They also believed that a simple democratic system often falls short of this idea because of factions that amount to a numerical majority. Therefore, most of them concluded, a republic must protect the legitimate interests of a minority against the whims of a selfish majority.

So, the real question was: What counted as a true minority interest? The small-state delegates believed that the states had meaningful differences among them, so they deserved protection. The large-state delegates thought they did not. It was not so much a philosophical debate, but an empirical one. Did the states count as distinct communities that deserve protections in an otherwise democratic system?

In the end, the small states won the debate by wearing the Constitutional Convention out. It was not the strongest advocates of proportionality that gave way. Men like Madison opposed equal apportionment in the Senate until the end. Instead, it was moderate delegates from the large states who turned the tide. Early on, for instance, well before the arguments grew heated, Pierce Butler of South Carolina argued it was necessary to "preserve" the "balance and security of interests among the states." That was an important, albeit subtle, concession to the point made by the small states.[29] Likewise, Nathaniel Gorham of Massachusetts saw "some weight in the objections of the small states," which inclined him "to a compromise as to the rule of proportion."[30] George Mason of Virginia noted that, generally speaking, the delegates thought "the faculty of self-defense" was necessary for "an efficient government," and he was inclined to give the small states such a power, "as he conceived" them "to be essential" to the Union.[31] Eventually, delegates like these capitulated when they saw how serious the small-state delegates were.

And so was born the so-called Great Compromise—the proportional House and equal Senate. It is also known as the Connecticut Compromise because it was first proposed by Sherman and helped along to fruition by Oliver Ellsworth, both of Connecticut.

What of this bargain? Obviously, it was necessary as a matter of expedience. There was no getting the small states to agree to the Constitution without it, and there would be no country as we know it today without the small states. Population or not, you cannot have a country with just Massachusetts, Pennsylvania, and Virginia. But does equality among states in the Senate stand up according to the principles the framers agreed on? The small-state delegates believed that equality in the Senate was necessary to protect their interests and thus to promote government by consensus. Were they correct?

Probably not, in 1787 at least. For how obsessed the framers were with the tamping down of factions, American citizens at the time of the Constitutional Convention, though diverse in many cultural respects (especially regarding religion, about which there was a wide array of opinion in America), were pretty equal in terms of property ownership, relative to Europe. They were also generally engaged in farming land that they owned themselves. Charles Pinckney of South Carolina put it thusly:

> The people of the United States are perhaps the most singular of any we are acquainted with. Among them there are fewer distinctions of fortune and less of rank, than among the inhabitants of any other nation. Every freeman has a right to the same protection and security; and a very moderate share of property entitles them to the possession of all the honors and privileges the public can bestow: hence arises a greater equality.[32]

There were not yet meaningful distinctions between classes of the citizenry. So one could look at the population in, say, Pennsylvania and compare it reasonably well to Delaware. And Madison and Hamilton were right that, insofar as different economic and social interests existed, they cut across state lines, undermining the chances of the large-state alliance that delegates from small states feared.

But Pinckney believed that "this equality is likely to continue," and on this count he guessed wrong.[33] Indeed, even as several large-state delegates were denying a difference of interests with the small states, they were fretting over the potential admission of new, smaller states in the West. That was a sign that they understood that *someday* large and small states could have distinct interests. Hugh Williamson of North Carolina, for instance, claimed that "he could not comprehend how the smaller states would be injured" in a proportional Senate, yet he also warned about the unique problems posed by future states from the West.

> They would be small states, they would be poor states. They would be unable to pay in proportion to their numbers; their distance from market rendering the produce of their labour less

valuable; they would consequently be tempted to combine for
the purpose of laying burdens on commerce and consumption
which would fall with greatest weight on the old States.[34]

Gouverneur Morris of Pennsylvania was likewise worried about the
Union being flooded by the "range of new states which would soon be
formed in the West." It was necessary "to secure to the Atlantic states a
prevalence in the national councils," lest they be overwhelmed by these
western states that "will know less of the public interest . . ., will have an
interest in many respects different," especially in "involving the community in wars" whose "burdens and operations . . . would fall chiefly on the
maritime states."[35] Elbridge Gerry of Massachusetts also feared the West
in a purely democratic system and warned about "putting ourselves into
their hands."[36]

As Madison and Hamilton predicted, interstate divisions among the
13 original states in the early years under the Constitution would usually
involve questions of commerce or slavery, which cut across small and large
states. But Morris, Williamson, and Gerry were also prescient. The future
states of the West would have distinct interests, would at first be smaller,
and would become a major political faction by the 1810s. Ironically, delegates like John Dickinson, Bedford, and Paterson were right, but for the
wrong reasons. They were not really defending the interests of their own
states, but those of the yet unformed western states.

It is also of great historical importance, for the Senate more than any
other institution facilitated the American settlement of the West. From
the western perspective, joining the Union under the terms of the Constitution was an impossibly good deal, much better than making a bid for
independence or aligning with a foreign power. Once admitted, a western
state would gain not only the American military's protection but also two
senators, enough to guarantee its perspective would not only be heard in
Congress but reckoned with. In a purely proportional system, becoming a
state would have been tantamount to submitting to rule by the "Atlantic
states," as Morris called them, for they held the balance of power for much
of the 19th century. Who is to say what the states in the West would have
done without the Senate? Would they have aligned with Spain or Mexico?
Would they have struck out on their own? These are questions that were

rendered moot thanks to the Great Compromise. The putative rebellion of the West is the proverbial dog that never barked in American history, because the Senate gave the region a meaningful share of lawmaking power.

This is far from the only time when the Senate helped mediate factional disputes that overlapped with geography. By the 1830s, the Senate's partiality toward sparsely populated states maintained the balance between free and slave states. This was exactly the opposite of what many large-state delegates had expected in 1787. They thought that Virginia, North Carolina, and Georgia would be drivers of population growth. But immigration, industrialization, and a more appealing climate in the North facilitated the expansion of the free states, such that by the 1830s, Ohio—which did not even become a state until 1804—rivaled Virginia in its political power. Amid this surprising imbalance in population, the Senate kept the political equilibrium between the slave states and the free states.

Though slavery is a moral blight on our history, we must acknowledge that the South never gave that vile institution up willingly, through the political process. It had to be stripped from Dixie by military force. When the North first gained the population advantage in the House, it still lacked the industrial capacity to wage what would become the Civil War. The South rebelled in 1860–61, in part because it realized that it was powerless to stop an all-northern coalition from controlling the government—a coalition that could have formed decades earlier in a purely proportional system of representation. If the South had rebelled much earlier, it likely would have been better able to fight the North to a draw and negotiate its exit as an independent, slaveholding nation. The Senate, by keeping the South in the Union longer, helped delay the war until the North could prevail.

After the Civil War, the Senate played an important role in the political divide between the agricultural and industrial factions. Great Britain was already going through the early stages of the Industrial Revolution when the delegates met in Philadelphia. Within 30 years, it would begin to cross the Atlantic to the United States, profoundly altering the social, cultural, and economic foundations of the country. Industrialization would go hand in glove with rapid urbanization, and soon population centers such as Boston, Chicago, Detroit, New York, Philadelphia, and Pittsburgh would become larger than anybody thought possible in 1787. Meanwhile, other areas would remain fundamentally rural and agricultural—particularly in the South and later across the Great Plains.

Thus, state populations would come to reflect legitimate differences in economic ways of life, creating meaningful "rivalship of commerce, of manufactures," as Bedford put it. Rural America dominated the small states, urban America the large.[37] This created geographical divides on multiple issues, such as railroad regulation, currency management, and tariff rates. Without the Senate, the predominantly rural and agricultural states of the Great Plains and Mountain West would have had no meaningful voice in the political process. Thanks to the Senate, they did.

Today, the Senate continues to protect the interests of rural people— and not just their economic uniqueness but also their cultural views and social norms, which can be distinct from urban and suburban residents. Just as 150 years ago, life in rural America is different from life in urban America, and the Senate makes sure that both sides have a voice in government. It is not that these rural communities get to dictate policy to their larger, urban counterparts. It is rather that the latter cannot tell the former what to do. By giving voice to less populous communities, the Senate forces policymakers to account for their interests, to reconcile them to those of more populated centers, and to forge compromises that are geographically broader than they would otherwise be in a purely proportional system.

Thus, what became apparent in the working out of history—which was only dimly evident to the delegates in Philadelphia in 1787—is that equal apportionment of the Senate is good for consensus. It has "extend(ed) the sphere" of policymaking, to borrow a phrase from Madison—first by protecting western interests from those of the Atlantic, then the slaveholding South against the free North, and later the agricultural and rural interests against the urban and industrial ones.[38] It does not do this perfectly, of course. Delaware is still a small state, but it has mainly been reduced to a suburb of Philadelphia; meanwhile, Texas and California are large states that have both urban and rural areas. Still, the Senate does capture part of this difference, and it forces compromises between geographically distinct groups of people. The Senate may not be a democratic institution, but it has proven itself to be a republican one, for it helps build consensus in the lawmaking process.

* * * *

There was widespread agreement at the Constitutional Convention that a single person should wield the executive powers of government. Just as the modern corporation requires a CEO to make sure things get done, the United States of America needed somebody to enforce the laws and command the military. The framers gave this officer a decidedly unflashy title—president, which historically meant the person who presides over a meeting—because they did not want to conjure images of a king. Still, they knew they needed somebody who could take responsibility. As President Harry Truman said, "The president—whoever he is—has to decide. He can't pass the buck to anybody. No one else can do the deciding for him. That's his job."[39]

The American president does not simply enforce the laws. He plays a role in making them, through the presidential veto, a power whose origins trace back to the British system of government. As the British Constitution evolved over time, the legislative power had come to be vested in the Parliament, but the king had the power of an absolute veto. If he rejected a law, Parliament could do nothing. However, in practice, this power had become a nullity in Great Britain by the time the US Constitution was being drafted. The last time any British sovereign withheld royal assent was Queen Anne in 1708.

This makes the American adoption of the veto peculiar. Why would the framers give such a power to the American president, after it had been basically unused in their former motherland for 80 years? This was especially strange considering colonists were frustrated by the way the king used his royal authority to reject laws passed by their colonial legislatures. In the Declaration of Independence, for instance, Thomas Jefferson complained that George III had "refused his Assent to Laws, the most wholesome and necessary for the public good."[40] Why give the president the opportunity to do likewise?

Alexander Hamilton offered guidance on this question in *Federalist* 70, the most important in his series on the executive branch. "Energy in the executive is a leading character in the definition of good government," he argued. Only the vigorous use of executive authority could defend the country from foreign attacks, administer the laws in a steady manner, protect private property, and stand athwart "the enterprises and assaults of ambition, of faction and of anarchy."⁴¹ This was a not-so-subtle dig at the parochialism of legislative assemblies, where small-minded politicians representing local interests were known to scheme and connive against the public good.

The veto is thus another way to enhance the prospects of consensus in the lawmaking process. The president is the only nationally elected office-holder in the federal government with any real power. (The vice president is elected as well but only has the authority to break ties in the Senate.) Senators and representatives, by contrast, represent just a segment of society—their states or their districts. The president alone claims the country at large as his constituency, and the framers expected he would wield the veto to protect the national interest. This is an important, final safeguard to protect the nation from unfair or partial legislation.

The president's role in the legislative process is limited. He only gets an up or down vote on a whole piece of legislation after it has passed both chambers. That constrains him from haggling over the nitty-gritty details, which are left up to the House and the Senate. Instead, the president is supposed to keep an eye on the big picture, to make sure that the compromises that Congress fashions still work for the good of the whole country. Congress could, after all, cobble together a majority in favor of a bill through an alliance of factions all looking out for themselves, rather than the national interest. In today's parlance, this kind of legislating is called "logrolling," in which legislators trade votes so that they can send benefits back home to their localities. While sometimes a matter of political necessity, this style of lawmaking can be contrary to the public interest, which is when the president is supposed to come in with his veto.

The president is thus a guardian of the national interest in the legislative process, preventing the law from benefiting factions at the expense of the good of the entire nation. Hopefully, such alliances will be broken through the back-and-forth of politics between the House and the Senate, but if not, the president is there to step in. This also helps explain why his veto is not absolute but can be overridden by a two-thirds majority in both chambers. It is highly unlikely that such a large coalition in both chambers of Congress represents a purely factional interest. It is more likely reflective of the national interest and thus has the power to pass laws over the president's objections.

* * * *

Popular sovereignty over the legislative process is essential to a republic. It is the way in which the people truly rule themselves. But, as we have seen, a simple democracy is prone to democratic tyranny, where a majority governs for its own interests rather than the whole community. The framers sought to counter that tendency through the idea of consensus, forcing majorities to become larger, broader, and more considered than those in a strictly majoritarian system.

In practice, consensus makes for a complicated and elaborate lawmaking process. But it is purposeful. The House and the Senate mirror public opinion, albeit in different ways, meaning that governing coalitions in Congress reflect a wide diversity of interests. And the president, as a constitutional officer with a national constituency, can guard the public interest with his veto power. With so many different factions having the power to determine which bills become law, it is unlikely that a single, hegemonic interest will emerge. What happens next is an elaborate process of bargaining, negotiating, and politicking, as the various interests in government struggle to find common ground. The compromise position they can live with hopefully reflects the consensus view of the nation.

Naturally, no system of government is without its trade-offs. In founding the Constitution on the principle of consensus, the framers sacrificed other advantages that might come through more democracy. Was this a wise decision? That is the topic of the next chapter.

5

The Necessity of Consensus

In June 2016 the people of the United Kingdom shocked the world and transformed the international landscape by voting to leave the European Union by a margin of 52 percent to 48 percent.[1] That vote set off a chain reaction that ultimately swept out two British prime ministers—David Cameron and Theresa May. Finally, Prime Minister Boris Johnson brokered a deal with the European Union to secure Britain's economic and political independence from the continent.

Such a dramatic policy change could never happen so quickly in the United States. The British government as it has evolved over the past 200 years is effectively a unicameral system, in which the people rule through the House of Commons. This is what enabled such decisive action: The Commons set the plebiscite, the majority spoke through it, and thereafter, the Commons pursued Brexit until it was achieved. In our system, not only does no one institution have such sweeping power, but a narrow, 52-48 majority is rarely sufficient to bring about decisive change. Instead, our Constitution is premised on the idea of consensus, whereby the government usually takes action only when it is approved (or at least not objected to) by a large, broad, and considered majority.

Which type of system is preferable? Progressive critics, following in the steps of Woodrow Wilson, have long argued that the British system makes more sense, for it clearly expresses the public will and induces government action accordingly. Yet this is what makes the Brexit vote so interesting, as progressives—certainly in the United Kingdom but also here in the United States—thought Brexit was a bad idea! It just goes to show that no system of government is perfect. There are trade-offs to be made regardless of what we choose.

Admittedly, a system built on consensus creates several significant problems. First, policy outcomes are often inefficient, as bargains must be struck with factions to garner their support. Second, the demands of consensus make it more difficult to address public problems quickly, even when the status quo is clearly no longer viable. Third and most danger-ously, consensus can, in some instances, make it more difficult for citizens to secure their rights.

Despite these weaknesses, consensus holds a decisive advantage as the foundation of our government. The United States is too large and diverse to be organized under any other principle. In a free society, obedience to the state depends on the consent of the governed, which requires that people feel they have meaningful participation in the regime. By forcing coalitions to be larger, broader, and more considered, consensus can offer that kind of public buy-in.

* * * *

The standard of consensus requires that a multitude of factions be brought into a governing coalition to enact laws. But what happens when factions are indifferent to an issue or have alternative policy priorities? Rather than negotiate on the general parameters of the issue at hand, they might instead demand side benefits for themselves as a condition of their support. That generates inefficiencies in public policy, increasing its cost, making it overly complex, and, in extreme examples, undermining the public interest the policy is meant to advance.

Several examples illustrate this point. In the early 1780s, the Continental Congress was consistently strapped for cash, and nationalists like Robert Morris of Pennsylvania proposed an impost of 5 percent on imported goods, implemented by the state governments but with the funds earmarked for Congress. Many states balked at this, and in response to their hesitancy, James Madison—at that point a young delegate from Virginia—proposed a number of "baits" to get them to agree: The Continental Congress would, in exchange for enacting the impost, provide a series of benefits for the states. For instance, to small states like Maryland with no access to western territory, Madison promised to finish nationalizing the western lands. To war-weary states like Virginia, Madison promised an abatement on overdue requisitions to Congress. The idea was that, while states would support the impost for their own interests, the overall agenda was good for the country. But side deals such as these are often too complex to manage. The nation-alists could never simultaneously get all 13 states and the Continental Con-gress to agree to any plan, and the project fell apart by 1784.

A more recent example involves "earmarks," a term of art employed to describe the practice of Congress directing public funds for specific projects. Earmarks enable legislators to claim credit for bringing resources to their home states or districts. By the 1980s, congressional leaders realized they could be a tool to encourage members to support big, "must pass" pieces of legislation, such as authorizing federal transportation spending. The problem with earmarks was that, as members realized they would be rewarded if they threatened to withhold support from necessary legislation, they began to do so en masse. Between the 1990s and early 2000s, the number and cost of earmarks grew rapidly, attracting widespread public outrage until they were prohibited a decade ago (until being restored by the Democratic-controlled House in 2022). Earmarks are basically a matter of waste or inefficiency. The government still gets its essential business done; it just costs more than it otherwise would.

Sometimes, these "logrolls"—where policymakers support each other's parochial initiatives—go from being merely complex and inefficient to downright harmful. American industrial policy between the War of 1812 and the Great Depression is a case in point. During this period, the country pursued protectionist policies, imposing heavy taxes on imported goods. In their early incarnation, tariffs on imported goods probably helped the country, as nascent American industries struggled to compete with their more advanced British counterparts. But as the industrial sector matured, protective tariffs did little good. American industry did not need protection from foreign competition, and the wage benefits gained by laborers were canceled out by higher prices for consumers. Yet Congress consistently resisted reform, as members sought to claim credit for delivering benefits to their constituents. The way for a congressman or senator to secure protection for their community's industry was to trade support with other members. As a consequence, the tariff became a complicated tangle of inscrutable rates on all manner of goods, without any rhyme or reason beyond political calculations.

Worse, there were two significant instances when tariff logrolls gravely damaged the national interest. The Tariff of 1828 united the West, mid-Atlantic, and New England around exorbitant rates that placed economic costs on the South, a region that had no need for protection and had to suffer substantially higher prices on imported goods. This tariff precipitated the Nullification Crisis of 1832–33, in which South Carolina claimed that the law was unconstitutional and thus of no force in the state. In 1930, amid the Great Depression, the Republican-dominated Congress turned to industrial protection as a tonic for the nation's ills, thinking higher tariff rates would boost wages for workers and stabilize the economy. Contemporary economists know the strategy was foolhardy, for it amounted to a giant tax hike during an unprecedented economic collapse. But the execution of the plan turned out to be especially dangerous. Members of Congress scrambled desperately to secure bounties for the industries in their states or districts, transforming the bill into a massive logroll that hiked tariff rates to unprecedented levels. President Herbert Hoover signed it into law, and the Depression worsened.

* * * *

The most frequent complaint about our system of government is probably that things never get done. While that is an exaggeration, it is fair to say that our system has a status quo bias, which favors the current policy over any given alternative, even if there is agreement that the situation needs to change. A large swath of the country might believe that a given reform advances the public good, but because the coalition supporting change is not quite large enough, the status quo endures.

The status quo bias has been a common problem in American political history, as it has often taken a crisis to generate enough support to solve lingering policy problems. As noted in Chapter 1, the Constitution was born of such a crisis moment. After years of incompetence and indecision, the Continental Congress endorsed the plan for a constitutional convention only in the face of Shays's Rebellion. Likewise, the slavery issue came to the forefront when Missouri asked for admission to the Union as a slave state in 1820, but it lingered unresolved for more than a generation, as there was no majority of sufficient size and breadth to make a final determination on the matter. It was not until after the Bleeding Kansas crisis of 1854 that the North and West began to unite in opposition to slavery's spread, leading to the election of Abraham Lincoln.

After the Civil War, the country saw similar patterns of punctuated equilibria regarding the emergence of the modern administrative state, government regulation of business, and the provision of social welfare.

The story was typical across all these policy domains; years of inaction would finally be broken by some sort of crisis. The assassination of President James A. Garfield in 1881 marked the beginning of the end of the old spoils system and laid the foundation for a professionalized bureaucratic class. The assassination of President William McKinley inadvertently ushered in the Progressive Era, as his successor Theodore Roosevelt rallied the nation to the cause of reform. The Great Depression ended a conservative revival and brought about the New Deal. The assassination of John F. Kennedy gave Lyndon B. Johnson a sufficiently broad mandate to enact the Great Society. Outside these moments of crisis, the wheels of politics tend to grind slowly.

This is partially a consequence of the demands of consensus. It is not sufficient for a majority, even a sizable majority, of factions to agree that the current policy regime is unacceptable. They must, rather, agree that a given alternative is preferable to the status quo. That is often easier said than done among diverse economic, social, religious, and political groups. More often than not, a substantial minority is bettered by the status quo and will fight through the political process to retain it.

The best contemporary example of this problem is arguably Medicare. In their rush to expand access to care during the Great Society, Lyndon B. Johnson and his congressional allies enacted a program that was far too generous to the private sector and wealthier seniors, ballooning costs for the government and distorting the market for medical care. Multiple factions on the left and right have long acknowledged that the status quo is faulty. However, there is hardly consensus on what reforms to implement. And even if there were agreement between the country's public intellectuals, any policy alternative would have to overcome a powerful phalanx of interest groups—doctors, hospitals, insurers, senior citizen advocates, and so on—before it could be enacted. Given the history of American public policy, it is a fair bet that the country will continue merely to tinker at the margins of this problem until its costs become so great that reform becomes unavoidable.

The American government tends to underreact, doing nothing while the costs of inaction accumulate, followed by an exuberant burst of policymaking that is sometimes poorly conceived, generating new problems for subsequent generations. Modest, frequent changes to public policy could be much more efficient, in multiple ways. They would address emerging problems in a timelier manner. They would enable greater experimentation in policy alternatives, promoting the discovery of superior solutions. They would prevent the accumulation of costs over time from manifestly failed status quo policies. They would minimize the consequences of bad decisions, as policies can be more easily revised later. But the demands of consensus make it extremely hard for the government to act in this manner, and bad policies tend to stick around for generations.

* * * *

If a consensus-based system can protect status quo policies that are not conducive to the country's general welfare, it can also in some instances undermine the provision of justice. This is tragic, for justice is government's central purpose, and the consensus system was adopted largely to secure it.

The animating idea behind consensus is that a large, broad, and considered coalition will usually only form around fair ideas, thus preventing any group from having their rights violated. But what happens when the people unite around unjust sentiments? Obviously, in those circumstances, consensus will fail to secure justice. Of course, the same problem would similarly affect a simple majoritarian system. The difference is that it would take a smaller shift in public sentiment to secure justice in the majoritarian government than it would in the consensus government. In a system requiring something more than a majority to alter the status quo, the aggrieved minority must persuade many more of its fellow citizens of the justice of its cause.

Madison only dealt with this problem tangentially in *Federalist* 10, his most comprehensive statement on consensus. He presumed a raucous political back-and-forth, in which citizens vie for advantages from the government and block other citizens' efforts. But, per Madison, this only created a "tendency to break and control the violence of faction."[2] It might not stop factionalism, but Madison did not elaborate on when or how it might fail. History has shown that one point of failure is when the issue turns on who is considered a citizen. This itself is an inherently political question fraught with all sorts of distributive implications—for expanding the number of bargaining factions decreases any individual group's ability to acquire benefits for itself.

At the time Madison wrote *Federalist* 10, the full rights of citizenship were extended to white male property holders, although the trend was moving in the direction of all white men having the franchise. The cheapness of western territory made the property-holding requirement less burdensome in the early 1800s, and by the time of the Civil War, property requirements had mostly been eliminated. Thereafter, from a Madisonian perspective, white men formed a majoritarian faction in society, with a shared interest in maintaining exclusive political power. True expansions of the franchise beyond this were few and far between during the 19th century. The 15th Amendment, which granted African Americans the right to vote, was not ratified until 1870, and Wyoming became the first territory to grant women the right to vote in 1869. Even then, these rights were often paper-thin. Women did not gain the nationwide right to vote until 1920, and the first significant civil rights legislation after Reconstruction was not enacted until the 1960s.

To be sure, women and racial minorities would always have faced a hurdle in persuading such a faction to recognize their rights in a system of simple majoritarianism. However, in our consensus-based system, the hurdle was substantially higher. All these changes required constitutional amendments, combined with enacting legislation by Congress. Indeed, major breakthroughs in civil rights tended to follow moments of crisis. By framing World War I as a fight to save democracy, President Wilson inadvertently gave a marketing edge to the suffragette movement. And the assassination of Kennedy just months after he endorsed civil rights reforms spurred the nation into enacting landmark legislation that might otherwise not have passed.

This problem endures even as women and African Americans have entered the body politic. We might say that those living today are a majority faction, whose interests are aligned against those of the unborn and, by extension, the greater body politic as it exists through time. The unborn cannot participate in civil society and have no recourse to object to the massive public debts being incurred in the present age, which they will be obliged to pay off. They also cannot register their objections to abortion, which violates their natural rights. Likewise, upon conviction, prisoners lose many of their procedural rights, including the rights to vote, to assemble, to privacy, and most obviously to bear arms. Yet they do not surrender their natural rights. How then are they to defend them against, for instance, inhumane or dangerous prison conditions? How can they protest the aggressive and potentially unfair use of plea agreements by the government? They must depend on other factions taking up their cause. Perhaps in a more narrowly majoritarian system, the interests of these groups might be better secured, as half plus one of today's electorate might be inspired to protect them, but alterations to the status quo in our system require a much larger and broader majority. Thus, their interests are more easily ignored.

* * * *

The problems of inefficiency, gridlock, and the persistence of some forms of injustice are manifestations of the general weakness of a consensus-based regime. It is not expeditious. A system built on simple majority rule can act much more quickly and efficiently than one such as ours.

So to return to the Brexit example, the United States would not be able to extricate itself from an organization like the European Union as easily as Great Britain did. There would be no popular plebiscite to give such immediate legitimacy to the move. Rather, the public's preferences would have to be expressed through the regular process of electoral politics, in which the two parties would run on a whole host of issues, and thus no clear mandate for Brexit might emerge. And even if it did, that preference would have to be expressed in both congressional and presidential elections, for the president in our system is tasked with negotiating international treaties. Any such deal would then have to get the approval of two-thirds of the Senate. That threshold could be especially difficult. The Scots and the Northern Irish opposed Brexit, while the Welsh were lukewarm in their support. In the United States, such regional variations would probably mean the Senate would struggle to ratify such a treaty.

Insofar as we think only of good policies that the United States government is unable to implement because of the demands of consensus, the more narrowly majoritarian system of Great Britain certainly seems superior. The people spoke, and the government acted. Our people speak, and quite often nothing happens—because they do not speak loudly enough,

enough of them do not speak, or some well-placed faction objects to their call for action.

But as the old saying goes, the grass is always greener on the neighbor's yard. While it is easy to lament our government's inability to enact changes expeditiously, consensus is nevertheless essential to our system. By forcing governing coalitions to be larger, broader, and more considered than in a simple majoritarian system, consensus creates opportunities for citizens to meaningfully affect public policy. In a country as populous, geographically vast, and diverse as ours, this is the best way, and perhaps the only way, to secure popular support for the government.

To appreciate this, it is worth returning to the political thought of Madison—in this case, the essays he wrote in the early 1790s as he was waging partisan warfare on behalf of the new Republican Party against the emerging Federalist Party of Alexander Hamilton. In an essay for the *National Gazette* titled "Spirits of Government," Madison argued that governments could be "properly divided, according to their predominant spirit and principles into three species of which the following are examples."[3] The first, Madison noted, was a "government operating by a permanent military force, which at once maintains the government, and is maintained by it; which is at once the cause of burdens on the people, and of submission in the people to their burdens." This is the type of government, he noted, "under which human nature has groaned through every age."[4] The second type is an oligarchy that operates

> by corrupt influence; substituting the motive of private interest
> in place of public duty; converting its pecuniary dispensations
> into bounties to favorites, or bribes to opponents; accommo-
> dating its measures to the avidity of a part of the nation instead
> of the benefit of the whole.[5]

This government, Madison argued, was an "imposter" to a true republic, his third type. A republic is

> a government, deriving its energy from the will of the society,
> and operating by the reason of its measures, on the under-
> standing and interest of the society. Such is the government for

which philosophy has been searching, and humanity been sigh-
ing, from the most remote ages.[6]

It was, Madison noted, "the glory of America to have invented, and her
unrivalled happiness to possess" a true republican government.[7]

But what, it must be asked, is the "will," "understanding," and "interest"
of American society? At the time of our nation's founding, the people were
divided along religious, cultural, ethnic, linguistic, and geographic lines,
even as most citizens were generally in the same socioeconomic condition
of being small farmers. Our nation became substantially more diverse over
the subsequent centuries, beyond what anybody in 1787 could possibly have
imagined. We the people of 2023 are not anchored by a shared language, race,
gender, ethnicity, religion, culture, sexuality, economic vocation, or even history among our many types of citizens. Indeed, it is staggering to think of
just how many different types of people call themselves American today.

Contrast our diversity to many European nations. When the English
looked upon Queen Elizabeth II, for instance, they could trace the history of a distinct group dating back to the Norman Conquest; through the
Middle Ages, the religious wars of the early modern era, the emergence of
the constitutional monarchy, the growth of empire abroad and democracy
at home, and the struggle against totalitarianism in the 20th century; and
finally into the present. Americans do not, have never, and cannot possibly
ever have a shared identity like this.

What then keeps a "people" such as the Americans—who really, by the
strict understanding of the term, are nothing of the sort—together? This
question is really a matter of how loyalty is generated within a regime.
Return to Madison's typology. A government run by military force induces
loyalty to the state through the fear of violence. A government run through
bribery uses monetary rewards to create loyalty. A republican government
induces loyalty because the people believe the law reflects their interests,
values, and perspectives. The problem is that in a republic like ours, no
single set of values embodies the entire nation. So loyalty to the government must come from the belief that one gets to influence the formation
of law. The process itself takes on signal importance in securing the bond
between citizen and state in a country. We are held together by the shared
commitment that each of us gets a say in the direction of the nation.

A simple majoritarian system is too likely to leave many of us on the outside looking in, which would produce a sense of alienation from the government, striking at the very foundation of republicanism. It is not enough for people merely to have the right to vote. If people feel as though the franchise is pro forma and meaningless because they are locked in a permanent minority, they will feel frustrated, anxious, and angry. Recall from Chapter 4 the comments of William Paterson at the Constitutional Convention on the prospect of the colonies having representation in Parliament. It "could not have been . . . more than one-third of the number of representatives," meaning that America would have no real say at all. Paterson preferred the rule of a "despot" over such a democratic tyranny.[8] This is a universal sentiment. How long would a minority of citizens consent to be governed by a majority whose values and interests are contrary to their own? Whatever the answer is, it cannot be indefinitely. Eventually, loyalty to the regime will have to be purchased through bribery or coerced through the threat of force.

Contrast that to a system built on consensus, in which a majority must be larger, broader, and more considered to get things done. The scope of meaningful participation will be much larger. People will feel a greater sense of ownership in the affairs of state; perhaps it does not reflect my values all the time, but it does some of the time. While few people are entirely satisfied with the actions of the government, few people are entirely dissatisfied. Consensus increases the chances that more people score policy victories over time, which creates a sense of ownership of the nation, and therefore loyalty to it.

This need is of heightened significance in a geographically large nation such as the United States. While we are diverse on a national scale, we are more likely to be homogenous on a statewide and especially local level. In a system founded on simple majoritarianism, geographically concentrated factions remote from the seat of government are bound to be the most sensitive to rule by a distant and "foreign" power, which might seem indifferent and downright hostile to their values. The government's authority therefore must be distributed with particular sensitivity to sustain the loyalty of far-flung locales, for they are the most likely to waver and thus require military force to secure it.

Geography is of central importance in maintaining the Union. Consider once more the Constitutional Convention and the claims of the small states. Ultimately, the large states acceded to their objections because, without them, there would have been no country. Massachusetts, Pennsylvania, and Virginia were by far the largest states, but they were noncontiguous. The large states needed the small states in 1787, just as industrial America in the 19th century needed agricultural America, and just as coastal America needs "flyover" America today.

More broadly, every group in this country needs every other group. We often do not recognize that—thanks to our essentially selfish natures—but the economic vigor, the international strength, and the internal cohesion of the Union requires all of us to find a way to coexist with one another in political society. And because of our diversity, this can only happen through a careful distribution of sovereignty across multiple factions. In a word, it requires consensus.

It can be easier to notice the problems of our system of government than its virtues, especially when we compare it to other nations or when we think retrospectively. Looking back on the past, we can be easily struck by the country not doing the sorts of things it should obviously have done. But the virtues of the system are somewhat harder to detect. Human beings tend to assume that everything should go smoothly, an amazing propensity considering how often we are disappointed. When things go well, we are more likely to take it as given, failing to fully acknowledge the confluence of factors that led to the right result.

So perhaps the best way to appreciate the necessity of consensus is to return a final time to the Brexit vote. While the English are a distinct people, the United Kingdom of Great Britain is more of a polyglot, stitched together out of disparate peoples with distinct histories. As mentioned earlier, Scotland voted overwhelmingly against leaving the European Union. But because Scotland represents less than 10 percent of the national population, its judgment was overruled in the national plebiscite. Yet Scotland represents nearly one-third of the entire landmass of the United Kingdom. It has a unique history, culture, and set of interests. And the Scots—deeply frustrated by Brexit—might someday exit the United Kingdom. In 2014, a popular plebiscite in Scotland on the question of independence returned a vote to stay 55–44—a shockingly narrow margin in historical context, considering that England and Scotland have been joined for more than 300 years. As of this writing, the Scottish National Party, which favors independence, controls the Scottish Parliament and holds 44 seats in the House of Commons. If the Scots hold another plebiscite on leaving the United Kingdom, nobody can know what they will say.

In the United States, a region of Scotland's size and its distinct interests would probably be able to block an initiative like Brexit. As such, there are no "independence" movements in the United States, because there is no need for them. Our commitment to the idea of consensus makes sure that all voices have a meaningful say in the formation of public policy. It may make our system more inefficient, but consensus is the sine qua non of the American union. The nation would not, could not, exist without it.

* * * *

A government built on consensus has clear downsides. It can be inefficient; as factions haggle for their own advantage, the cost of doing the necessary business of the public can increase. It can favor the status quo too heavily; even as most factions agree on needed policy changes, the threshold might be too high to achieve the goal. Worst of all, it can be especially unfair to those minorities who are excluded from civil society; they must struggle all the more to convince a supermajority of citizens to permit them to enter.

Despite these substantial problems, the upside of consensus has a profound and decisive edge in a nation like ours. The distribution of power in a government built on consensus binds otherwise dissimilar people to the state. All free governments depend on the consent of the governed, and in a diverse society—where the people defy any systematic categorization—consent requires the widespread feeling among different people that they play a role in creating the law. That can only happen through consensus, whereby governing coalitions are larger, broader, and more considered than in a simple majoritarian system. This is of such importance that it is hard to imagine a nation like the United States ever coming into being, let alone sustaining its existence for centuries, without consensus as its foundational principle.

Let's turn now to a final issue surrounding consensus. In our system, built on the idea of large, broad, and considered majorities, it can be extremely difficult to effect change not just to policy but to the Constitution itself.

That means the people of today are bound by rules that were set hundreds of years ago. Is that consistent with a republic? Should the dead effectively wield such power over the living? That is the subject of the next chapter. .

6

Dead-Hand Control?

The First Congress of the United States began in April 1789, meaning that as of this writing, the Constitution has been in operation for more than 234 years. To be sure, there are institutions of government throughout the world that are older than this. King Charles III, for instance, can trace his ancestry back to the Anglo-Saxon House of Wessex. But of course, the nature of the British monarchy has evolved over the years. On the other hand, the United States House of Representatives of today is still the same House from 1789, institutionally speaking.

Our written Constitution is a product of the unique historical circumstances that brought the United States into existence. In overthrowing King George III, the Americans were forced to establish a new government out of whole cloth, and during a war no less. Contrast this to the British system of government, with its unwritten constitution that evolved over millennia according to political exigencies. The Americans did not have the time to wait for this to happen. An army had to be raised, and a war had to be fought—hence, the Articles of Confederation, drawn up in 1777 as the first American system of government. A decade later, the failures of the Articles of Confederation had become intolerable, which led to the Constitutional Convention. So the United States was bound to be "locked" into a written instrument of government.

This raises important questions that we in the 21st century should consider. The Constitution is old, but is it too old? Is the advanced age of the Constitution to be celebrated because it is a good instrument of government that facilitates public and private liberty? Or are we unfortunately saddled by "dead-hand control," the rule of a founding generation that has now been gone for nearly two centuries? Perhaps most important, does the fact that the Constitution was ratified by men who denied the rights of women or enslaved people render it out of date for the present age?

Answering these questions requires us to consider the amendments added to the Constitution, the crucial relationship between the doctrine of consensus and the stability of the foundational law, and the extent to which the Constitution is severable from those parts of it that denied rights to minorities and women.

* * * *

The framers never presumed that they would have all the answers to the problem of government, so they left two paths to amend the Constitution—a convention of the states (like the Constitutional Convention of 1787) and a process of congressional proposal and state-legislative approval. Since the creation of the Bill of Rights, embodied in the first 10 amendments, the Constitution has been amended only 17 times. The most drastic changes have been in extending the rights of citizenship to groups excluded by the founding generation. Otherwise, reforms have tended to be narrowly tailored to address specific problems.

Two of the 17 amendments responded to adverse Supreme Court decisions. The 11th Amendment overruled *Chisholm v. Georgia*'s declaration that states do not enjoy sovereign immunity from suits in federal court brought by citizens of other states. The 16th Amendment overturned the Court's decision in *Pollock v. Farmers' Loan and Trust* that an income tax was unconstitutional. Two others, the 18th and 21st Amendments, negated each other—with the 18th Amendment outlawing alcohol and the 21st Amendment repealing the 18th. That leaves 13 amendments to consider.

Seven of these amendments have expanded the sphere of civil society beyond the narrow scope created in the Constitution of 1787. The 13th, 14th, and 15th Amendments freed enslaved men and brought them into the constitutional system with the full rights of citizenship, although this promise would not begin to be realized in a durable way until the mid-1960s, with the passage of the Civil Rights Act and Voting Rights Act. The 24th Amendment, which outlawed the poll tax, eliminated a Jim Crow–era tactic by which racial minorities could be effectively excluded from politics. The 19th Amendment extended the full rights of citizenship to women. The 26th Amendment extended those rights to 18-year-olds. And the 23rd Amendment gave presidential voting rights to those living in the District of Columbia.

That means just six amendments have altered the structure of the government itself—and five of the changes have been relatively narrow. In response to the contested election of 1800, the 12th Amendment altered the Electoral College, including the elimination of the rule that the second-place finisher in the presidential election becomes the vice president. The 20th Amendment reduced the time between the election and inauguration—a response to the lengthy lame-duck presidency of Herbert Hoover during the Great Depression. The 22nd Amendment enshrined in law the precedent George Washington established of a two-term limit for the presidency, which had been broken by Franklin Roosevelt, who won four consecutive terms. The 25th Amendment clarified the order of succession for the presidency, on which the Constitution was silent. Meanwhile, the 27th Amendment is a true peculiarity. One of the original amendments in the Bill of Rights, it regulates congressional pay—but had laid dormant for over 200 years until it was revived for discussion in the 1980s and ratified in 1992.

So of the 17 amendments enacted since the Bill of Rights, just one has amounted to a drastic structural reform of the constitutional order—the 17th Amendment, which instituted the popular election of senators. In so doing, it did away with a founding skepticism of democratic institutions. This was not a decision taken lightly by the American people but rather a deliberate response to widespread and long-standing political corruption. Following the Civil War, senators became de facto bosses of their state governments and—largely immune from public oversight—were free to act on behalf of corporate interests on the federal and state levels. By the early 20th century, widespread disgust with the Senate's unresponsiveness to public demands led to this sweeping change.

The relative scarcity of major reform by amendment might suggest the Constitution's structure is reasonably sound. The relationship among Congress, the president, and the courts has required some tweaks at the margins—but just one fundamental reimagining in the direct election of senators. This is a sign of success. On the other hand, a critic might respond that the real problem is that it is too hard to amend the Constitution. Amendments require a national supermajority—two-thirds in both houses of Congress and three-fourths of the state legislatures. Popular demands for reform simply cannot cross the threshold needed to enact an amendment. As an example of this, one might point to the failure of the Equal Rights Amendment to be ratified despite overwhelming support in the 1970s. This is perhaps a sign that the Constitution is too anchored in the old ways, resistant to legitimate calls to update the regime.

The objection boils down to the problem of dead-hand control. We are bound by the instrumentalities of government created by men who have all been dead since 1836 (when James Madison, the last of the framers, died). That presents a challenge to the very notion of republican government, which is bottomed on popular sovereignty. Who exactly is sovereign? In some respects, it is a people who have been gone for more than two centuries.

Ultimately, dead-hand control is not an evil plot by the American framers. It is, rather, a consequence of the need in 1787 for a written constitution and the framers' commitment to the doctrine of consensus. They had no choice but to write an instrument of government. They could not wait the centuries it would take for one to evolve through the give-and-take of politics. Moreover, they were obliged by their political principles to make it difficult to change, absent a large, broad, and considered majority that reflects the public consensus. All in all, this is not a bad thing. No doubt, there are downsides, as ways of doing political business become outdated yet cannot be amended easily when there is no consensus on an alternative. Still, our written, generally fixed Constitution has provided the United States with many blessings, three of which merit special consideration.

First, the long age of our written Constitution has inculcated a sense of reverence that promotes social stability. Human beings are, as Alexander Hamilton once put it, "reasoning [rather] than reasonable animals for the most part governed by the impulse of passion."[1] The maintenance of society thus depends on not only "necessity" and "natural inclination," as David Hume argued, but also "habit."[2] Specifically, per Hume, "Men, once accustomed to obedience, never think of departing that path, in which they and their ancestors have constantly trod, and to which they are confined by so many urgent and visible motives."[3] As Madison argued in *Federalist* 49, "The reason of man, like man himself, is timid and cautious, when left alone," but it "acquires firmness and confidence" when it is fortified by "*antient* as well as *numerous*" opinions. (Emphasis in original.) Thus, even "the most rational government will not find it a superfluous advantage to have the prejudices of the community on its side."[4] Habituation limits the range of options the human mind might contemplate and over time creates a sense of reverence and respect for the established order. It thus keeps people from ruining the good aspects of society in a fit of passion, thinly justified by rational arguments.

Second, our Constitution has a nice combination of rigidity and flexibility. On the one hand, it creates clear lines of authority that regulate behavior among governing elite. The ancient Roman constitution was unwritten and depended heavily on norms that the elites were merely expected to follow, which they began to ignore toward the end of the republican era. While norms are important in American governance, ultimately the fundamental rules of the game are clearly established by the written Constitution. On the other hand, the framers strategically and cleverly used ambiguous phrases in the Constitution to make it a little bit supple. For instance, Congress possesses the power to regulate "interstate commerce."[5] What exactly does that entail? The Constitution does not say and instead allows for the political process to determine its meaning. Likewise, Congress is allowed to collect taxes for the "general welfare,"[6] another term of notable vagueness. It has the power to do anything "necessary and proper"[7] to bring its other powers into effect. It guarantees the protection of "due process,"[8] an idea that evolves with the times. The Eighth Amendment outlaws "cruel and unusual punishment,"[9] a term whose meaning likewise changes with the ages.

So while the Constitution creates clear lines of authority on the most fundamental levels, particularly war and peace, its vagueness allows for flexibility on specific policy questions. Our history is full of such disputes, dating back to the debate over the Bank of the United States, chartered in 1791. Washington thought carefully about whether the Bank was constitutional under the necessary and proper clause, a phrase whose meaning is far from self-evident.

Likewise, there have been debates about the constitutionality of any number of powers, including federal spending on internal improvements, the income tax, the New Deal, and the Civil Rights Act. This provides Americans with the best of both worlds. It is almost like the reason to build a skyscraper out of steel. It is strong enough to hold the massive weight of the building but pliable enough that it will not topple over in bad weather.

Third, and perhaps most important, a system built on consensus must rely on fundamental laws that are difficult to change. The framers believed the way to preserve republican government from corruption into mob rule was to favor large, broad, and considered majorities. It stands to reason that the bigger the change to be made to society, the greater the consensus must be. And there is nothing bigger than changing the Constitution, since it sets the very rules of the political game.

The alternative would scarcely be tolerable. If the Constitution were easy to change, and a factional majority rewrote it to its advantage, the problems would be catastrophic. In fact, we saw a version of that during Prohibition, an initiative of the rural, Protestant America against urban Catholics. The result was widespread disregard for the law, criminal behavior, and heavy-handed federal enforcement. Imagine reapportioning the House or altering the rules of presidential selection to favor one faction or another. The document would change again and again, as narrow, temporary majorities would successively change it to their preferences. The result would severely damage public respect for the Constitution and degrade the sense that everybody meaningfully participates in the lawmaking process, which, as noted in Chapter 5, is essential to preserving the Union.

* * * *

The Constitution undoubtedly was, in its origins, a racist document. It legitimized the continued enslavement of African Americans and granted slaveholders political and legal advantages beyond what owners of other property enjoyed. The Civil War amendments removed these defects from the Constitution, and the civil rights legislation of the postwar era has in many respects made good on those promises. Nonetheless, some progressive critics of the Constitution see racism embedded much more deeply in the document and argue these changes have not been sufficient. Rather, they see the Constitution as a continued bulwark against true racial equality in the United States.

In the lead essay of the *New York Times Magazine*'s "1619 Project," Nikole Hannah-Jones argued that "this nation's white founders set up a decidedly undemocratic Constitution that excluded women, Native Americans and black people, and did not provide the vote or equality for most Americans."[10] She claimed this was part of a long history that deeply embedded racism in American politics, culture, and economics. As for the text of the Constitution itself, whose authors studiously avoided using the word "slavery," Hannah-Jones approvingly quoted from the Anti-Federalist essayist known as "Centinel," who blasted the protection of slavery in the Constitution as "especially scandalous and inconsistent in a people, who have asserted their own liberty by the sword, and which dangerously enfeebles the districts, wherein the laborers are bondmen." He went on:

> The words dark and ambiguous; such as no plain man of common sense would have used, are evidently chosen to conceal from Europe, that in this enlightened country, the practice of slavery has its advocates among men in the highest stations.[11]

While Hannah-Jones did not make any specific recommendations about the Constitution, the implication of her essay is that the founding charter is still part of America's race problem.

Any defense of the Constitution on the issue of slavery must begin by conceding that Hannah-Jones is right in important respects. In its original design, the Constitution embedded the interests of the slaveholding faction in several substantial ways. Most significant was the three-fifths rule, which counted an enslaved person as three-fifths of a free person for congressional apportionment and direct taxation. This rule, based on the proposed tax of 1783, gave the states with disproportionately high numbers of enslaved persons (Delaware, Georgia, Maryland, North Carolina, South Carolina, and Virginia) a bonus in the House of Representatives. The enslaved could not vote, so this political power accrued to the whites. This bonus in the House was transferred onto the presidency via the apportionment of presidential electors. Each state received electors equal to their House and Senate delegates, meaning that, once more, the South received political power beyond what the North had.

The slaveholding faction's advantages in the Constitution also limited congressional powers. While Article I, Section 8 gave Congress the power to regulate commerce with foreign nations and lay taxes for the general welfare, the legislature was forbidden from regulating the international slave trade for 20 years and was permanently enjoined from placing taxes on exports—a boon for the southern economy, which relied on exporting tobacco, indigo, rice, and cotton. The allowance of the slave trade also extended southern political power in Congress. While some southern states, such as Virginia, had already banned the trade, Georgia and South Carolina had not, so they were able to grow their political power by importing enslaved persons from Africa.

Noxious as each advantage was on its own, they compounded on each other in a foul manner. The founders embedded a version of the cruelest kind of oligarchy into an otherwise republican constitution. Southern wealth was transformed by the Constitution into political power, contrary to the principles of democratic republicanism to which most of the framers held. And this was a wealth that depended on denying the God-given rights of the enslaved, who had been kidnapped from their families; displaced from their traditional religions, languages, and cultures; and shipped across the world in a harrowing journey to a place they were hated, reviled, and abused.

Even worse is that most members of the Constitutional Convention knew slavery was fundamentally contrary to the principles of liberty to which the country was dedicated, but they went along with it. Perhaps the most disheartening moment of the entire Constitutional Convention came when James Wilson, a staunch advocate of the rule of the people, noted that he could "not well see on what principle the admission of blacks in the proportion of three fifths could be explained. Are they admitted as citizens? Then why are they not admitted on an equality with white citizens?" Yet in the next breath, he offered, "These were difficulties however which . . . must be overruled by the necessity of compromise."[12]

The racism of the founders—proclaiming the "necessity of compromise" on a matter as essential as human freedom—drives the critique of Hannah-Jones and others who have made the same point. However, even though the history is undeniable, its implications are not. Is the Constitution hopelessly befouled by the racism of its authors and the economic structures for which it offered political protections? If so, that suggests a kind of philosophical exclusionary rule: Ideas derived from a racist society are a priori contemptible or at least highly suspect. That is a very sweeping implication and must be considered carefully.

Racism is an especially virulent and pernicious manifestation of factionalism, which is a consequence of the selfishness embedded in the human character. Our inclination to place ourselves at the center of the moral and physical universe, and our analogous tendency to elevate our desires above the good of all, leads us to join with others who are "like us." Racism has long been a convenient way to sort "us" versus "them," for one faction to dominate another, and ultimately for individuals to secure their interests at the expense of others' rights.

Only recently has Western civilization begun to explicitly disavow racism. Raced-based slavery was legal throughout much of the West until the middle of the 19th century. Even after formal abolition, European powers continued a kind of de facto slavery through their colonial projects, while the southern United States did likewise through its system of segregation. It was not until the 20th century that these social and economic hierarchies really began to break down, and it was only after World War II that a psychological rejection of racial hierarchies has been effected in younger generations. These are all positive developments, and this process must continue, including in the United States. Systematic inequalities remain between those of European ancestry and those descended from enslaved people, and insofar as those are consequences of the law, the law must be altered.

Nevertheless, throwing the Constitution into the dustbin of history because of its racist origins is a profoundly radical idea. Must old ideas be abandoned or otherwise cast into doubt because the originators of past achievements held views that are now understood to be noxious? Such a standard would isolate the contemporary West from the accomplishments of most of its history. This is more in line with the Jacobinism of the French Revolution or the Marxism-Leninism of the Russian Revolution than the common ethos in liberal nations such as the United States, where knowledge is assumed to build through accretion and mistakes are corrected over time.

Moreover, if we accept the founders' view on factionalism as an expression of human nature, this progressive critique implies a continuous revolution. The civilizational calendar will have to frequently be reset to a proverbial "Year 1," as the old ways are inevitably discovered to have been tainted by human selfishness. Racism—or for that matter sexism, homophobia, or any dislike of another for group characteristics—is a manifestation of that quality endemic to human nature. Factional chauvinism is not going anywhere, nor are whatever justifications we come up with to rationalize it. We are probably acting in discriminatory ways right now that we refuse to acknowledge but a future generation will. That means that we, too, will have to be denounced, just as we must denounce the founders. And so it goes for every generation. How then can learning ever accrue, or real progress ever be made, if one is persistently required to reject the past for being hopelessly benighted?

A more sensible point of view is to acknowledge that the framers got some things tragically wrong but some things spectacularly right, to distinguish carefully between the two, and to fix the former while retaining the latter. The framers' great success was their effort to develop a stable and republican system of government in which political power is shared by free and equal *citizens*. Their great failure was to define citizenship in too narrow of terms, mainly male property holders of European ancestry. The latter mistake does not render the former accomplishment invalid. Instead, we should acknowledge that *within* the scope of citizenship as defined in 1787, the American constitutional order was the most bracingly egalitarian attempt at self-government in modern history. And importantly, it is still an effective structure for securing consensus in the policy process among citizens. The solution therefore is not to reject the Constitution, but to broaden the ambit of those who count as citizens within it. And indeed, the country has done precisely that, expanding the scope of citizenship dramatically.

None of this is to suggest that the Constitution, or the laws of this country in general, no longer have provisions that might be racist, sexist, homophobic, or otherwise bigoted. The point, rather, is that arguments to that effect cannot rely exclusively on a general indictment of the sins of the past. A careful, empirical argument must be made.

To appreciate this, consider one of many recent criticisms of the Constitution based on the matter of race. In a 2019 essay for the *Atlantic*, Wilfred Codrington III of Brooklyn Law School and the Brennan Center extended Hannah-Jones's general critique to argue that the Constitution's original racism not only poisoned the Electoral College then but does so today as well. He argued that the Electoral College was a "Faustian bargain" that the North negotiated with the South. Even though "populations in the North and South were approximately equal," a popular vote for the presidency would give the South less clout because of its "considerable, nonvoting slave population."[13]

At first glance, the Electoral College appears to be an example of how the racism of the Constitution was *severable* from its non-racist aspects. There is nothing inherently racist about apportioning electors by state, equaling the number of senators and representatives. In fact, even without racial considerations, there is a good chance the founders would have adopted some institution like the Electoral College. The Constitution, after all, is a compact among the citizens of the separate states, and having resolved disputes over the allocation of congressional power through the Great Compromise, it made sense for the founders to apply the same logic to the selection of the president.

So how is the Electoral College still racist? Per Codrington: "The current system has a distinct, adverse impact on black voters, diluting their political power." There is a substantial African American minority in some white-majority states—such as Alabama and Mississippi—and "their preferred presidential candidate is virtually assured to lose their home states' electoral votes."[14]

Codrington's argument takes us far afield from the intended racism of the document at the time. Now, we are in the domain of political science, trying to identify effective racism in the present. And on this front, the evidence does not favor Codrington's thesis. For starters, it is a state legislature's choice to award electors on a winner-takes-all basis, which all states except Maine and Nebraska do. In states like New York and Maryland, this works to African Americans' advantage, as they can align with white Democrats and dominate the states. In other states, like Alabama and Mississippi, it works to their disadvantage, with white Republicans holding the balance of power alone.

Characterizing the Electoral College as continuously racist becomes even more difficult when we consider historical episodes when it enhanced the political bargaining power of African Americans. After the Civil War, the Electoral College was an institution that induced northern Republicans to expand the political rights of the freedmen. Once the three-fifths clause was repealed by the 13th Amendment and African Americans counted as full citizens for the purposes of apportionment, the southern states returned to the Union with *more* political power than they previously wielded. This created a problem for northern Republicans. Their fear, which was reasonable, was that southern secessionists would reacquire political control of their states and use their additional votes in the House and the Electoral College to retake control of the federal government. This was a big reason the Radical Republicans pushed for the 14th and 15th Amendments: to ensure that the freedmen would get to participate in the government as a check against the former secessionists. These amendments form the legal bedrock of the modern Civil Rights Movement.

More recently, African Americans' migration into northern cities between World War I and World War II was an indirect cause of the massive civil rights gains in the subsequent decades—again, conditioned by the politics of the Electoral College. In the 1940s and '50s, states such as Illinois, New York, Ohio, and Pennsylvania were hotly contested between Democratic and Republican presidential candidates. That made African Americans, despite their relatively small share of the electorate in those states, enormously important. The prospect of winning the African American vote is one reason New York Gov. Thomas Dewey—a civil rights reformer for his day—won the Republican nomination in 1944 and 1948. The GOP was desperate to get back into political power and looking to attract northern African Americans to its banner. This in turn prompted the Democrats to adopt a civil rights plank to their 1948 platform. Both parties began to campaign actively for the African American vote, which contributed to the dramatic civil rights triumphs of the 1960s.

Today, African Americans still wield enormous political power in several states despite their relatively small shares of the electorate, again because whites are roughly evenly split between the parties and the state's electoral votes are winner takes all. Nowhere is that more the case than Pennsylvania, where the white population is not nearly as Republican as in Alabama. Consequently, African Americans—particularly in Philadelphia, Pittsburgh, and Erie—have proven integral in electing Democratic statewide officials and securing the state's electors for Democrats in most presidential elections in the past 30 years.

Even in strongly Republican states with large minorities of African Americans, the Electoral College can redound to their political power in surprising ways. African American voters dominate the Democratic presidential nominating process in the strongly Republican states of the Deep South. Since 1992, the Democratic candidate that southern African

Americans supported has won the nomination in five out of six contested nomination battles—Bill Clinton in 1992, Al Gore in 2000, Barack Obama in 2008, Hillary Clinton in 2016, and Joe Biden in 2020. The reason for this is that the apportionment of party delegates partially mimics the apportionment of electors to the Electoral College, so southern African Americans wield outsized power during the nominating contests.

The point of this discussion is not strictly to single out Codrington, although his argument is deeply flawed. It is to demonstrate that it is extremely difficult to identify structural, systemic, or intrinsic racism in the Constitution with the Civil War amendments now enforced and African American participation at all-time highs. Yes, in some times and in some places, African Americans might be in political situations that limit their power under some constitutional provision. But in other times and other places, that same provision might provide advantages.

That the framers were originally racist does not alter how we should evaluate the Constitution today. Perhaps the taint from the early days has not fully been removed from the Constitution, but arguing that it remains requires careful articulation of systematic problems, not general denunciations and the selective marshaling of facts. If African Americans (or women or any other group previously not given the full rights of citizenship) were still excluded from political life, that would be another story. But they have since been included.

* * * *

Ultimately, we the people are not so much bound by the framers' instrument of government as we are by their standard of consensus. And as Chapter 5 argued, for all its faults, consensus is an essential ingredient to a country as large and diverse as the United States of America. The Constitution can be scrapped if a large, broad, and considered majority has come together on an alternative. While this creates a form of dead-hand control, it is worth remembering that this is exactly the standard to which the founding generation held itself. The Constitution only became the law of the land when nine of 13 states ratified—a supermajority. Moreover, ratification by both Virginia and New York (the 10th and 11th states, respectively), while not technically necessary for adopting the Constitution, was crucial to its long-term success.

Those possessed of the spirit of Jacobinism will not be persuaded by this argument. Over the generations, many intellectuals, activists, and ordinary citizens have expressed supreme confidence in humanity's ability to remake itself, virtually from scratch. Our Constitution is premised on a different view of human nature, one that calls for caution. Whereas today's radicals see a fundamentally flawed and backward document, those of us who understand humanity as the framers did see in the Constitution a reasonably effective instrument of government that, by virtue of its age, provides a bulwark against the dangers of sweeping social, economic, and political disruptions.

7

The Parties

A t first glance, political parties fit uneasily within our constitutional system. "We the people of the United States, in order to form a more perfect union," as the preamble puts it,[1] seems hard to square with what we today call the tribalism (or what the framers would call factionalism) of the modern parties. Parties labor for the benefit of their supporters, often against the good of the whole or the rights of their opponents. That is not how republican government is supposed to work, is it?

The framers certainly thought so, and many of them were surprised when, by 1795, the body politic had essentially organized itself into two distinct political parties—the Federalists and the Republicans (or what we today remember as the Democratic-Republicans). Except for a brief period between roughly 1816 and 1825, parties have been the vehicle through which American politics happens.

Over the past 60 years, political scientists have identified several ways that parties can facilitate representative government. By controlling the legislature, they overcome the collective action problem inherent to large organizations. By creating interbranch alliances among fellow partisans, they facilitate the enactment of legislation. By controlling political nominations, they regulate elite ambition. By building large networks of donors, they mitigate the financial burdens candidates face in mounting campaigns. By providing voters with information, they help make vote choices more rational and electoral outcomes more predictable.[2]

Without disputing these advantages, it is important to note that American parties as they exist now were generally not developed in a purposeful fashion. Rather, they evolved as a response to short-term problems politicians faced at various points in the republic's history. Many of the benefits the parties supply to republican self-government are actually side effects rather than the direct intention.

Many, but not all. In fact, the earliest instantiation of a national political party—the Republican Party of Thomas Jefferson and James Madison begun around 1791—was done quite intentionally. The purpose of the Republicans was to alert the nation to the dangers of what they believed was a dangerous faction, later named the Federalist Party, and rally the public to defeat this anti-republican force. In this way, the Republican Party served a role in promoting consensus, by informing voters of what was happening in government and helping them reach a more considered and mature conclusion. Today, parties can still enhance democratic accountability in this way, making them an essential, extra-constitutional element of our republic.

* * * *

The United States was not the first country to develop a party system. That distinction belongs to England. The Tory and Whig parties were born of the English succession crisis of the 1660s, with the Whigs calling for the exclusion of the Catholic James, Duke of York, from the throne and the Tories defending his claim. These two coalitions proved lasting, and by the time of the American Revolution, the Tories generally represented the landowners and members of the Church of England, while the Whigs represented British merchants, industrialists, and nonconforming Protestants.

Most of the framers ascribed the existence of the British parties to the defects of their system of government. The Americans thought the parties were only sustained by royal patronage, in which the king's ministers bought off members of Parliament to vote against their constituents. The Constitution denied such powers to the American president, so the framers figured that factional disputes could be resolved without the recourse of party.

But that is not what happened. In fact, many of the same men who designed what they hoped would be an anti-party Constitution in 1787 were enthusiastically engaged in partisan conflict within a decade. Integral to this development was Madison. His Republican Party, as he called it, was the country's first modern political party, which, according to political scientist V. O. Key Jr., includes three main components: a party in government, a party organization, and a party in the electorate.[3] This party did not come to exist all at once, and at no point did Madison or Jefferson elaborate an explicit theory of party, but the maturation of the Republican Party progressed over the 1790s.

The party in government was, at first, centered around Madison in the House of Representatives, and as early as the Second Congress, an identifiable coalition was responding to his direction. By 1792, Republican leaders were coordinating among the states (particularly Virginia and New York) to nominate a candidate to challenge John Adams for the vice presidency. This process was further refined such that Jefferson and Aaron Burr were nominated for the Republican ticket by the congressional caucus in 1800.[4]

Public administration was also susceptible to partisan control. Although Jefferson was not aggressive in trying to purge his political opponents after he took the presidency, he was keen to restore balance between Republicans and Federalists throughout the government (which, by his view, was an approximately two-to-one or three-to-one ratio in favor of the Republicans) and reward those party leaders who were crucial to his election. He accomplished this by removing Adams's last-minute appointments, dismissing the fiercest Federalist partisans, and replacing marshals and attorneys to compensate for the Federalist tilt of the Supreme Court. All this served to integrate the branches of government under Republican auspices, corralling the federal authority that the Constitution had originally dispersed.[5]

Party organization—usually in the form of correspondence committees and nominating conventions—also developed briskly during this period, although there were striking differences in sophistication from state to state. New York and Pennsylvania took an early lead, and by 1800, both had relatively advanced operations in place to select candidates, communicate the party message, and deliver the vote. The Republicans' superior organization was essential to their victory in 1800. They made their biggest move in New York, where the electors would be chosen by a joint session of the state house and senate. New York City's at-large state senate delegation was the focal point of the campaign, and Burr—an intrepid and innovative organizer of the Republican interest—was crucial in nominating a slate of esteemed candidates and then turning out the party vote.[6]

The central means for cultivating a partisan spirit in the electorate was the Republican press, which Madison was again at the center of. He and Jefferson induced the former's college friend, Philip Freneau, to publish the *National Gazette*, initiating a proliferation of Republican papers—such as the Philadelphia *Aurora*, the Newark *Centinel of Freedom*, the Pittsburgh *Gazette*, and later the *National Intelligencer*. The Republican press was so pervasive that by 1800, Federalist Sen. Uriah Tracy of Connecticut would lament that there was a Republican paper "in almost every town and county in the country."[7]

Madison has often been accused of inconsistency between the time he wrote his *Federalist* essays in 1787–88 and his Republican period of 1790 and onward. During his Federalist period, he seemed to disdain parties as a form of faction, but in his Republican period, he extolled the virtues of partisanship.[8] What to make of this seeming contradiction? As historian Lance Banning has noted, we should not apply concepts and categories common to the current age back to the 1780s and 1790s in general and to Madison in particular.[9] Rather, he must be understood carefully on his own terms. When we take the time to appreciate how Madison perceived the political situation in the early 1790s, we can begin to understand that this seeming contradiction melts away and in its place appears an interesting and often overlooked function of American political parties.

In *Federalist* 10, Madison used the term "party" interchangeably with faction, which he defined as

> a number of citizens, whether amounting to a majority or minority of the whole, who are united and actuated by some common impulse of passion, or of interest, adverse to the rights of other citizens, or to the permanent and aggregate interests of the community.[10]

As noted in Chapter 2, *Federalist* 10 outlines Madison's idea of the extended republic, his main strategy for solving what he called at the Constitutional Convention "the inconveniencies of democracy" while remaining "consistent with the democratic form of [government]."[11] His idea was to create a large, diverse polity so that no faction could amount to a majority—thus preventing democracy from destroying the republic.

But what happens when a faction is a minority of the citizenry? In *Federalist* 10, Madison had little to say on the matter, brushing it aside with just a single sentence:

> If a faction consists of less than a majority, relief is supplied by the republican principle, which enables the majority to defeat its sinister views by regular vote: It may clog the administration, it may convulse the society; but it will be unable to execute and mask its violence under the forms of the constitution.[12]

He was relatively confident about the ease with which fractious minorities may be defeated, in part because the Americans had done away with the sort of established privileges that then existed under the British constitution. There was seemingly no place in the United States government for a minority to hide—at least not for long. The real danger facing the nation in 1787 was majorities run amok, not minorities. Madison was not alone in this view. Most of the debates at the Constitutional Convention revolved around how to design the government precisely so that majorities cannot destroy republicanism. Nobody in Philadelphia in 1787 was particularly worried about minority factionalism, more or less for the reason that Madison laid out in *Federalist* 10.

It was the success of Alexander Hamilton's financial plan that destroyed Madison's optimism about the power of the majority to root out dangerous minorities. The crucial moment in the early government for Madison was the publication of Hamilton's *First Report on the Public Credit* in the winter of 1790. Having been nominated to helm the newly created Treasury Department, Hamilton was tasked with submitting to Congress a program for handling the nation's public finances. Always one to take the bull by the horns, Hamilton used this assignment as an opportunity to introduce a sweeping vision for a new financial system. Over the next two years, beginning with the *First Report on the Public Credit*, continuing with the *Report on a National Bank*, and concluding with the *Report on Manufactures*, Hamilton would redefine the political debate in the United States as a referendum on the soundness of his economic agenda.[13]

The secretary's proposals amounted to a public-private partnership between the government and the commercial elites who owned most of the public debt.[14] Hamilton planned to offer them massive windfall profits—by granting a nearly full repayment of the domestic debts, both state and federal; allowing that debt to be used to purchase shares in the newly chartered Bank of the United States; and granting bounties and other forms of cash assistance to manufacturers and producers of raw materials. In this way, the secretary planned to emulate the financial system of Great Britain, whose innovations in public finance during the 18th century transformed the island nation into the world's dominant power.

Hamilton had good reason to expect support from his friend and ally Madison. The two had worked together on matters of public finance while serving in the Continental Congress in the 1780s. Yet the secretary was wrong. Madison not only opposed every one of Hamilton's proposals but also led the charge against them in the House of Representatives, where his formidable skills nearly scuttled the secretary's plan to assume the debts of the states.

Madison had three particular reasons for outrage. First, he argued that the policy benefits were distributed too lopsidedly. They all accrued to a narrow segment of society, mainly the commercial faction in the northern cities that had bought government debt in the 1780s.[15] Second, he believed that Hamilton's plan to charter a national bank was unconstitutional. The framers had not written such a power into the Constitution, and the ratifying conventions that adopted it believed congressional power was limited. Hamilton seemed to want unlimited power.[16] Third, Madison was deeply worried about the public-private partnership that Hamilton was creating between the government and the wealthy, especially through the Bank of the United States, which would be privately owned but hold public tax dollars. Madison warned that with all of its wealth, it could become a political force unto itself, a "powerful machine."[17]

Politically speaking, Madison threw everything he had at Hamilton's plan, but to limited success. Hamilton mostly carried the day. By the terms Madison had set forth in *Federalist* 10, this should not have happened. A minority, such as the one Hamilton supposedly led, might be able to "clog the administration" and "convulse society," but it should not be able to "execute and mask its violence," so long as the republican principle of majority rule was in place.[18] Yet Hamilton had won, anyway. It seemed that Madison had been too optimistic about the capacity of republican government to prevent minorities from taking control of the state. How had the Hamiltonians managed to do that? And what could Madison and Jefferson do in response? Madison's answers to these questions point toward his justification for party government in the United States.

* * * *

By the summer of 1792, Madison and Jefferson were nearly in a panic over the events in the national government. Hamilton's successes had led to a massive injection of fresh capital into the fledgling economy. A speculative bubble ballooned thanks in large measure to the machinations of William Duer, a friend of Hamilton and the first assistant Treasury secretary. Duer used his insider connections to try to corner the market on government debt. When his efforts failed, the bubble popped in what became known as the Panic of 1792, the first financial crisis of the new United States. As far as Madison was concerned, this was proof of the new, unholy alliance between government and commerce. As Madison warned Jefferson, the speculators were becoming "the pretorian band of the Government—at once its tool [and] its tyrant; bribed by its largesses, [and] overawing it, by clamours [and] combinations."[19]

By this point Madison had already been developing this argument in the pages of the *National Gazette*. Between November 1791 and December 1792, he offered 18 unsigned essays on a variety of subjects, such as immigration, money, and the ideal distribution of citizens in a republic. But time and again he returned to several themes that clarify why he and Jefferson were in the process of forming a political party.

A main topic for Madison was the threat Hamilton posed, although the secretary was never mentioned by name. Madison argued that Hamilton and his allies were "more partial to the opulent than to the other classes of society"[20] and had "avow[ed] or betray[ed] principles of monarchy and aristocracy."[21] Their goal was to replace the plain republicanism of the United States by increasing "*natural distinctions* favoring an inequality of property" and adding "to them *artificial distinctions*, by establishing *kings*, and *nobles*, and *plebeians*."[22] (Emphasis in original.) In this way, "The government itself may by degrees be narrowed into fewer hands, and approximated to an hereditary form."[23]

How did Hamilton intend to bring this about? One tactic was what Madison called "consolidation," or replacing the federal form of the Constitution with an omnipotent national government. Madison believed that such a system would inevitably favor the executive branch, as Congress could not manage the details of governing the whole nation. The growth in executive power would increase the "splendour and number of [the president's] prerogatives," further undermining Congress and "by degrees transform[ing] [the president] into a monarch."[24] And the only way Hamilton could accomplish what the Constitution manifestly forbade was by "arbitrary interpretations and insidious precedents, to pervert the limited government of the Union, into a government of unlimited discretion."[25]

Madison also believed that Hamilton's financial system had doubled as a source of patronage for the secretary to effectively buy off the people's representatives to support his schemes. Madison warned that the Hamiltonian system was

> substituting the motive of private interest in place of public duty; converting its pecuniary dispensations into bounties to favorites, or bribes to opponents; accommodating its measures to the avidity of a part of the nation instead of the benefit of the whole: in a word, enlisting an army of interested partizans, whose tongues, whose pens, whose intrigues, and whose active combinations . . . may support a real domination of the few, under an apparent liberty of the many.[26]

Essential to this project, Madison warned, was the "unnecessary accumulations of the debt of the Union . . . thereby [increasing] the causes of corruption in the government."[27] More debt meant more opportunities for speculation, more patronage, and thus more power for Hamilton.

How could Hamilton get away with this scheme under the republican principle of majority rule, which, as Madison had predicted in *Federalist* 10, should eventually drive a minority faction from power? In the *National Gazette*, he answered that his opponents were sewing divisions among the people. "The antirepublican party, as it may be called, being the weaker in point of numbers" had "strengthen[ed] themselves with the men of influence" and had taken advantage of "all prejudices, local, political, and occupational, that may prevent or disturb a general coalition of sentiments."[28] In this way, it was trying to make it "impossibl[e]" for the people to act together. Public "silence and insensibility" would leave "the whole government to that *self directed course*"—namely, what Hamilton and his clients desired.[29] (Emphasis in original.)

The way to combat this anti-republican force, Madison urged, was for the people to become politically engaged. They had "to guard and adorn the vital principle of our republican constitution."[30] Every citizen must "be at once a centinel over the rights of the people; over the authorities of the confederal government; and over both the rights and the authorities of the intermediate governments."[31] In "defending liberty against power, and power against licentiousness," the people could thwart the "partizans of anti-republican contrivances."[32]

Essential to this civic revitalization was for the people to recognize their shared interests. Even as Madison defended the federated nature of the Constitution, he believed that "the more readily" the people

> sympathize with each other, the more seasonably can they interpose a common manifestation of their sentiments, the more certainly will they take the alarm at usurpation or oppression, and the more effectually will they *consolidate* their defence of the public liberty.[33] (Emphasis in original.)

This required them to eradicate the kinds of "local prejudices and mistaken rivalships" that he believed the Hamiltonians were looking to exploit and instead "erect over the whole" nation "one paramount Empire of reason, benevolence and brotherly affection."[34]

In this way, the people could become like "Argus to espy" violations of their rights (Argus being the beast of many eyes from Greek mythology).

> Their eyes must be ever ready to mark, their voice to pronounce, and their arm to repel or repair aggressions on the authority of their constitutions; the highest authority next to their own, because the immediate work of their own, and the most sacred part of their property, as recognising and recording the title to every other.[35]

In the *National Gazette*, Madison termed this great mass of people the Republican Party, but his use of the word "party" here is not to be confused with the earlier notion of party that he disdained in *Federalist* 10. Indeed, in the *National Gazette* essays, he reiterated his point that though "parties are unavoidable" in every society, "the great object" of government must be "to combat the evil."[36] But this is not how he conceived the Republican Party, whose name had special significance in 1791–92. Madison's vision for this Republican Party was not of a faction, but rather a grand coalition, rooted in "a common sentiment and common interest."[37] Perhaps the best modern comparison would be the British unity cabinets headed by David Lloyd George during World War I and Winston Churchill during World War II.

The challenge, Madison believed, was getting the people to realize this— to look beyond their own parochial concerns, see through the Hamiltonian efforts to dupe them, and act in defiance. It was a problem as old as time, Madison believed. The whole history of government, he argued, had been one of "slavery" by the few over the many. When the people have been "ignorant—they have been cheated; asleep—they have been surprized; divided—the yoke has been forced upon them." How then do we make the people "enlightened . . . awakened . . . [and] . . . united?"[38] Madison argued that anything that "facilitates a general intercourse of sentiments" was useful for this purpose, for it would enable the people to recognize their shared interests. And to this end, he praised "good roads, domestic commerce, a free press, and particularly a *circulation of newspapers through the entire body of the people.*" These would, he believed, amount to an effective "contraction of territorial limits" and therefore be "favorable to liberty."[39] (Emphasis in original.)

Madison's advocacy of newspapers is especially noteworthy because the proliferation of newspapers was to become a key priority of the Republican Party. Moreover, the employment of nominating caucuses, circular letters, and congressional organization—all of which the Republicans embraced— served the same purpose. They effectively brought diverse factions of people together so they could recognize their shared interests and act in a coordinated manner to defend self-government.

Madison's list of grievances against Hamilton—his intentions, ambitions, and policy program—was overstated. Hamilton was not looking to establish a "monarchy bottomed on corruption," as Jefferson put it later.[40] It was a lamentable miscalculation that Madison made, one that he never acknowledged, even later in life when he had come to accept the soundness of much of Hamilton's economic program. Still, the secretary's system of public finance did produce corruption, as government insiders traded freely based on their advanced knowledge of the secretary's plans. The Panic of 1792 was caused by a speculative mania originating from Hamilton's confidant and former assistant Duer, and it was calmed only when the secretary basically agreed to bail the market out.

Setting aside whether Hamilton was leading a minority faction intending to destroy the republic, the important point for our purposes here is that Madison thought he was. And his response was to form a political party that informed voters of the danger, connected them to one another based on their national interests, and engaged them more fully in the political process.

From this perspective, we can appreciate an oft-overlooked value of political parties. Madison was confident in *Federalist* 10 that minority factions were little danger in a democratic republic. By 1791, he realized that elections were not enough to drive them from government. Sometimes, the people need be spurred to action. That is one job of the political parties. They can, at least in theory, enlighten, encourage, and mobilize the people to identify and oppose minority factions in government. They therefore give greater effect to the principle of majority rule.

To be sure, Madison's Republican Party is different than contemporary parties in several important respects. Relevant to this discussion, its originators did not see the party as one half of a system, whereby two or more parties offer different views of the public good and the voters select among the options. Instead, the Republicans saw themselves as representing the interest of the vast majority of the people (hence, their choice of name) and the Federalists (or as Madison called them in the *National Gazette* essays, the antirepublicans) as representing the interests of a small, wealthy clique. Still, this difference does not detract from the continuing relevance of Madison's basic point—that by sounding the alarm against government corruption, parties can help turn the people into a republican Argus, ever watchful for assaults on the constitutional order. To return to the original understanding of consensus—a majority that is larger, broader, and more considered than is required under a simple democratic system—parties at their best help public opinion become more considered, by equipping them with informational tools to keep watch over the government.

So by 1792, Madison had been instrumental in creating the two major institutions that protect republican government. The Constitution itself was designed primarily to minimize the threat of majority factions, which can be empowered by the principle of majority rule to govern for themselves at the expense of the whole or the rights of a minority. And the Republican Party was meant to have a countervailing effect, endeavoring to inform the people, bring them together, and make them vigilant against minority factions that employed "stratagem" to take over the government because they do not have the numbers for a straightforward political fight.[41]

* * * *

Unfortunately, today's parties do not reliably provide this kind of benefit. Rather than shining a light on interested factions controlling political power or resources for themselves, the Democrats and Republicans often facilitate them. This is due in no small part to parties, which were not written into the Constitution and have evolved haphazardly over the generations—often with an eye to serving the immediate needs of politicians, rather than the good of the nation. Sometimes, as in the case of campaign-finance reform, efforts to curtail party corruption or factionalism have inadvertently made matters worse. The so-called super PACs, or political action committees, that channel dollars from billionaire investors are, for instance, a consequence of the Supreme Court striking down portions of the Bipartisan Campaign Reform Act of 2002 as an unconstitutional limitation on free speech.

Ultimately, perhaps the greatest problem with our parties is that we do not see them in the way that Madison saw the Republicans. They are not, to earnest reformers of the political process, potential tools to educate the electorate and direct public energies in the proper directions. Rather, they are at best a nuisance to the republic or at worst the greatest threat to it. This is in error of which multiple generations have been guilty, reflecting a distinctively American distaste for partisan combat. We would be well-advised to listen to Martin Van Buren, one of the earliest and still most vigorous defenders of party government, who wrote:

> Political parties are inseparable from free government. . . . Doubtless excesses frequently attend them and produce many

evils, but not so many as are prevented by the maintenance of their organization and vigilance. The disposition to abuse power, so deeply planted in the human heart, can by no other means be more effectually checked; and it has always therefore struck me as more honorable and manly and more in harmony with the character of our People and of our Institutions to deal with the subject of Political Parties in a sincerer and wiser spirit—to recognize their necessity, to give them the credit they deserve, and to devote ourselves to improve and to elevate the principles and objects of our own and to support it ingenuously and faithfully.[42]

Van Buren's point illustrates how healthy parties are good for republicanism. The rule of the majority is not a sufficient condition for consensus, as so often majorities can be self-interested. But it is nevertheless a necessary condition. That's where the parties come in. They are useful for focusing the people's attention on the issues of the day, identifying candidates for office who will support the party's program, and making sure that the program is enacted once the candidates get in office. In a word, they can make public deliberations more considered than they otherwise would be. In this way, parties can enhance consensus, as the public become the Argus that Madison thought was necessary to keep watch over the republic.

8

The Judiciary

The United States Supreme Court wields sweeping powers today, but you would never know it just from Article III of the Constitution on the judiciary. It runs just 377 words long, less than one-fifth the length of Article I on Congress. Article III establishes the Supreme Court, outlines a process for choosing judges, delimits the boundaries between direct and appellate jurisdiction, and carefully defines treason and outlines the punishment for it; that is about it. Congress decides how many lower courts there shall be, how they will be organized, and even how many justices sit on the Supreme Court.[1]

It was clear to the framers that federal courts were necessary. Under the Articles of Confederation, state courts resolved disputes over the laws of Congress, so they naturally were partial to the states' interests. If the federal government were going to wield power effectively, it would need its own court system to punish violations of federal law. As James Madison put it, "An effective Judiciary establishment commensurate to the legislative authority, was essential." A government with a strong Congress but weak executive or judiciary "would be the mere trunk of a body, without arms or legs."[2]

Still, many Americans remained suspicious of the judiciary, so the framers decided that the less said, the better. Even within the Constitutional Convention, some delegates wanted to keep federal courts as limited as possible. For instance, John Rutledge of South Carolina thought the state courts could "decide in the first instance the right of appeal to the supreme national tribunal." Lower federal courts would make "an unnecessary encroachment" on state jurisdiction and create "unnecessary obstacles" to ratification.[3] But many delegates agreed with Madison that the judiciary had to be a complete branch. As a compromise, they let Congress handle the details.

Their ambiguity came at a price, however, for the vagueness of Article III created opportunities for the Court to expand its role. In due course, the Court claimed the ultimate power to interpret the final meaning of the Constitution, today called "judicial review," and eventually the scope of personal liberty itself. This makes it, for all intents and purposes, a lawmaking body in our constitutional system—which means it must be considered in the context of consensus-building.

The results of judicial review have been mixed regarding the matter of consensus. In most cases, the court acts as a neutral arbiter, standing above the political fray to resolve arguments between the branches and settle broader social controversies. But other times, it has taken sides in society, acting on behalf of some factions over others. In those instances, it is not merely interpreting the law, but writing it. That is because judges can be factional, just like everybody else. And American history is replete with examples of the Court imposing its own parochial values on the rest of the nation.

* * * *

The constitutional role of the federal judiciary has much in common with the president's power to take care that the laws are faithfully executed. After the law has been enacted, hopefully through a process that promotes consensus, its execution and adjudication should be value neutral. To that end, the framers hoped to establish a federal court system that was as independent of the political process as possible. Judges hold their office for life tenure, removable only by the impeachment power. Their salaries are likewise set by law and cannot be diminished. The idea is that they will be free to interpret and apply the law impartially, without interference from Congress or the president.

But this is still a republic, where all governing power is vested ultimately in the people. The framers employed indirect means to balance the demands of an independent judiciary with popular sovereignty. Congress cannot interfere with the work of judges, but it can structure the entire judiciary. Laws enacted by Congress established today's system of district and appellate courts, the size of the Supreme Court, and its discretion in hearing cases. And while judges are independent of politics after they are seated, they only arrive at their station after having been approved by the political branches. The president nominates judges, and the Senate approves them.

In *Federalist* 78, Alexander Hamilton sought to allay concerns that the judiciary would become tyrannical. Having neither "force nor will," as Hamilton put it, the court must depend on the other branches to effectuate its rulings.[4] The money to enforce its judgments must come from either Congress or the state legislatures. The enforcement power depends on either the president or state governors, meaning that multiple actors can stop a runaway court from imposing its will on the rest of the nation.

Importantly, the framers gave the Supreme Court the power to adjudicate "all cases, in law and equity, arising under this Constitution, the laws of the United States, and treaties made, or which shall be made, under their authority."[5] On one reading, the "case or controversy" clause, as it is known, suggests a straightforward and uncontroversial power. The courts are supposed to resolve disputes arising under the law, and the Constitution is the highest law, so it naturally follows that the courts must follow the Constitution.

But looking more closely at the phrasing, several questions emerge. What happens if a law contradicts the Constitution? Can the Court strike it down? What happens if the Constitution is unclear? Can the Court enforce its own interpretation? If so, far from being outside the political process, the court suddenly appears to be superior to it. Is that what the framers meant? This is the power of judicial review—or the idea that the Court has the unique privilege of holding the other branches accountable to its interpretation of the Constitution.

In most cases, judicial review is not a controversial matter at all. Cases are decided without entangling the courts in political issues, and the process plays out exactly as the framers hoped: Dispassionate judges make rulings based on the law rather than their political opinions, while juries deliberate based on the facts rather than their prejudices. Though far from perfect, the system is reasonably fair. Still, in a relatively small number of disputes, where the controlling legal authority is vague or contradictory, or issues of national importance hang in the balance, the contemporary Court can and does wield lawmaking power. Sometimes a federal law, state law, regulatory ruling, or executive order seems incompatible with the Constitution, and in those circumstances, the Court claims the right to strike down the acts of the other branches.

Some of the framers thought this was good. In *Federalist* 78, Hamilton boldly inferred that the Constitution gives the court the power to strike down unconstitutional laws. It cannot, Hamilton asserted, be "the natural presumption" that the "legislative body" should be the judge of its own powers. Instead, it is "far more rational to suppose" that the task would devolve on the court, "an intermediate body between the people and the legislature," protecting the former from the latter. "A constitution is in fact, and must be, regarded by the judges as a fundamental law," and "it therefore belongs to them to ascertain its meaning."⁶ This view did not sit well with Anti-Federalist critics of the Constitution. Melancton Smith, a New York politician writing under the name "Brutus," argued that Article III gave the court a "latitude of explanation" that it would use to tip the balance in favor of the federal government over the states. "In proportion as the former enlarge the exercise of their powers, will that of the latter be restricted."⁷

Madison was closer to Smith than Hamilton on this issue. Madison's *Federalist* 51 established the principle of checks and balances to not only regulate ordinary political conflict among elites but also police the constitutional order. The best way to settle arguments over the proper scope of each branch's powers was to set them against each other. Give each branch the power to defend itself, and the constitutional equilibrium would be maintained. Madison's Virginia Plan likewise embodied this notion of arbitration through politics. It included a "Council of Revision," which would have combined the president and select members of the courts to review congressional laws, ensuring that they pass constitutional muster. Madison also provided for the possibility of a legislative override of the council's judgments. Thus, constitutional questions would be resolved the same way that legislative compromises might be reached—through a well-organized political process that promoted give-and-take with the goal of achieving consensus.

While the framers discarded the Council of Revision, Madison still believed that politics was the proper way to resolve constitutional disputes. In 1789, as the House was debating whether the president had the power to remove executive officials, Madison argued,

> Nothing has yet been offered to invalidate the doctrine, that
> the meaning of the Constitution may as well be ascertained

by the legislative as by the judicial authority. When a question emerges as it does in this bill, and much seems to depend
upon it, I should conceive it highly proper to make a legislative
construction.[8]

In 1798, in opposition to the Alien and Sedition Acts, which effectively
criminalized political speech against the John Adams administration,
Madison authored the Virginia Resolutions, which called on the states to
"interpose" themselves between the people and this noxious act of federal
repression, an idea reminiscent of Hamilton's argument in *Federalist* 26
that the states would be "vigilant . . . guardians of the rights of the citizens" that could "sound the alarm" in the cases of federal "[e]ncroach-
ments."[9] Elaborating in 1800 about the role of the states in opposing
the Alien and Sedition Acts, Madison rejected the idea that the judiciary
had the sole authority to determine the Constitution's meaning. "There
may be instances of usurped power," he asserted, "which the forms of
the [C]onstitution would never draw within the controul of the judicial
department." Instead, "the decisions of the other departments" could
be "equally authoritative and final with the decisions of" the courts."[10]
Even in retirement, Madison still rejected the idea that the judiciary
alone should give meaning to the Constitution and argued instead that
legitimacy sprang from "the uniform sanction of successive Legislative bodies, through a period of years and under the varied ascendancy
of parties."[11]

Thomas Jefferson likewise rejected the idea that the judiciary was the
ultimate arbiter of constitutional meaning. In 1804, he wrote to Abagail
Adams, wife of former President John Adams,

You seem to think it devolved on the judges to decide on the
validity of the sedition law. But nothing in the [C]onstitution
has given them a right to decide for the executive, more than to
the Executive to decide for them. Both magistracies are equally
independent in the sphere of action assigned to them.[12]

Giving total power to the courts to decide the meaning of the Constitution would "make the judiciary a despotic branch."[13] Like Madison,

Jefferson believed that the Court should have a role in arbitrating disputes under the Constitution, but not the final role.

This vision of politics ultimately lost to a more Hamiltonian view, thanks to Chief Justice John Marshall, whose landmark *Marbury v. Madison* (1804) established for the Court a broad scope of authority. The circumstances of this case were hardly propitious for Marshall. He was a member of the Federalist Party, which emerged in the 1790s as a strong advocate for federal power and a tight alliance with Great Britain. After Jefferson's election in 1800, the political appeal of federalism rapidly declined. Recognizing that they had lost the support of the people, the Federalist-dominated Congress in 1801 tried to establish a permanent foothold in the courts. The Judiciary Act of 1801 greatly expanded the number of judges, and President Adams, who had lost the election to Jefferson, worked until the last night of his administration to get as many of his allies onto the courts as possible.

When the Jeffersonians took power, they engaged in a bit of political hardball. They not only repealed the Judiciary Act of 1801 but also refused to deliver the commissions that Adams had left behind. One of those was to go to William Marbury, nominated by Adams and confirmed by the Senate to be a justice of the peace in Washington, DC. All Marbury needed was his commission to certify his position on the court, but Madison, in his official capacity as secretary of state, refused to hand it over. Marbury sued to force Madison to act. Following the procedures created under the Judiciary Act of 1789, the case went directly to the Supreme Court.

Marshall was in a political bind. Clearly, Marbury was correct on the merits, but if the Court ruled for him, Madison would ignore it, and the Court's reputation would take a hit. Ruling for Madison, on the other hand, would look like an act of cowardice and yield the same result. It turned out, however, that Marshall was something of a Harry Houdini. He slipped free of his political constraints and offered one of the most ingenious rulings in Court history. He ruled for Madison, but it was the reasoning that mattered. Marshall argued that Marbury had no standing to take his case directly to the Supreme Court. Article III of the Constitution enumerates the types of cases in which the court has direct jurisdiction, and Marbury's was not one of them. The Judiciary Act of 1789 was therefore unconstitutional.

From a Madisonian standpoint, the notion of striking down the Judiciary Act of 1789 was problematic. The law by that point was 15 years old and had been uncontroversial. The political process had yielded a clear consensus on its legitimacy. But from Hamilton's viewpoint, as expressed in *Federalist* 78, the Judiciary Act was still fair game. It was the Court's responsibility to protect the people from legislative actions that violated the national charter. That the violation had happened more than a decade ago was no matter. Marshall's ruling was also a brilliant political maneuver. He delivered the Republicans a victory on the relatively insignificant matter of Marbury's commission, but he empowered the Federalist-controlled judiciary with an important authority. That he managed to do so at a moment when the Federalist Party was fading into political obscurity—it would cease to exist by 1820—is even more extraordinary.

Having established judicial review, Marshall refused to tempt fate with subsequent Republican administrations. Instead, he turned his attention to state laws, using judicial review to secure the federal government's supremacy in the constitutional order. By the end of his tenure, Marshall had presided over a dual revolution in American constitutionalism. He had established a broad understanding of federal power while minimizing the ways the states might interfere. He also elevated the court into the final arbiter of constitutional questions—just as Hamilton envisioned in *Federalist* 78. And he had done all of this with relatively little political controversy. He avoided jarring changes and instead employed a series of modest yet persistent nudges on the body politic. While the Republicans triumphed at the ballot box, Marshall worked behind the scenes to secure a legacy for Hamiltonian Federalism.

* * * *

Judicial review implies if not outright judicial supremacy, then a certain amount of finality. The Court claims the power to reject any law if a simple majority of the justices decides it violates its interpretation of the Constitution. No other branch operates so free of political constraints. In response to an adverse Court ruling, the rest of the government has but a few options, all of which are extraordinary: It can challenge the legitimacy of the Court, restrict its prerogative of judicial review, amend the Constitution, or change the Court's composition. Compare that to the relative ease with which the House, Senate, and president may check one another in the ordinary course of politics; all each needs to stop the others is simply to refuse to assent. To stop the Court, the rest of the government must coordinate, in what has often required a sustained and substantial effort. This is why, as Justice Joseph Story said, "the only check upon our own exercise of power is our own sense of self-restraint."[14]

From a Hamiltonian standpoint, this is nothing to worry too much about. The process of nomination and confirmation to the Court will hopefully elevate the best and brightest among the people, and such individuals of preeminence should have a broader scope of activity to interpret the law for the good of the public. Their self-restraint is a sufficient barrier. But from a Madisonian standpoint, the Court's separation from politics means that it is not bound by the constitutional structures that impose consensus on the lawmaking process. In most cases, the Court can be a dispassionate arbiter for justice because the interests and beliefs of the judges are not ensnared in the facts of the dispute. But when the Court takes on cases that have broader societal implications, Madison would argue it is much more difficult for judges to put aside their own partiality. The Court will be tempted to act like a faction—and something approaching a hegemonic one at that, for it is difficult for the other branches to resist its rulings through the constitutional mechanisms of politics.

Throughout Marshall's tenure, this was mostly an academic question. Madison personally disdained the way the chief justice would read Hamiltonian logic into the Constitution, but this hardly sparked broader social controversy. Marshall was equal parts smart, prudent, and purposeful, a true embodiment of the Hamiltonian elite. His involvement in the political process was laser-focused on federal-state relations, a subject that the average American would view as arcane. For instance, Marshall studiously avoided embroiling the Court in trickier questions about how individual rights might limit federal action. In *Barron v. Baltimore* (1833), he explicitly rejected the idea that the Bill of Rights restricted the state governments.

But what happens when those on the Court lack the sorts of extraordinary political virtues Hamilton praised and Marshall embodied? The answer, as illustrated several times in our history, is exactly what Madison would fear. The Court has periodically become a hegemonic actor, circumventing the political branches to impose its factional views of the public good on the rest of society.

The first and most regrettable example happened within a generation of Marshall's passing. By 1857, the slavery controversy was burning hot in American politics. The Compromise of 1850, which stitched together several proposals to find common ground between the North and the South, had failed to settle the matter. Southerners were angered that, with the admission of California as a free state, the North dominated the Senate and the House. Northerners were outraged by the Fugitive Slave Act, which strengthened the government's power to return escaped slaves to their southern captors. Matters grew worse with the Kansas-Nebraska Act of 1854, which allowed the territories of Kansas and Nebraska to decide for themselves whether to be slave or free. This led to outright violence in what came to be known as "Bleeding Kansas," further dividing the North from the South. It was in this fraught moment that a Southern-dominated Supreme Court issued *Dred Scott v. Sandford* (1857), the worst ruling in the judiciary's history.

Dred Scott was an enslaved man who had spent more than a decade in the free territories of the present-day Midwest. It was on that basis that Scott sued for his freedom in 1846. By 1857, Scott's case had worked its way up to the Supreme Court. Writing for a 7–2 majority, five of whom were southerners, Chief Justice Roger Taney struck two blows on behalf of the slaveholding interest. First, he argued that because Scott was African American, he could never be a citizen of the United States and thus could not file suit in federal court. Scott's supposed lack of standing should have been the end of the case, but Taney went on to argue that Scott's time in free territory was irrelevant. He was the property of his master, and the Fifth Amendment prohibits the seizure of property without due process of law. That had never happened, so Scott was still enslaved.

Taney's ruling was contemptible. The idea that an African American could not be a citizen of the United States was ahistorical and morally outrageous. And his expansive reading of property rights destroyed generations of carefully negotiated settlements between the North and the South. Taney blew all that up, arguing that enslaved persons were property wherever they go. In so doing, he foreclosed the possibility of future compromises over slavery and hastened the coming of the Civil War. The case made for bad law, bad history, and bad politics. It was pure, unadulterated factionalism; Taney and the southerners on the Court strained for a way to justify their region's interests, the welfare of the national community be damned.

In his first inaugural address, Abraham Lincoln flatly rejected the Court's authority to make such a judgment. While admitting that Court "decisions must be binding in any case upon the parties to a suit as to the object of that suit," he thought it absurd that "vital questions affecting the whole people . . . be irrevocably fixed by decisions of the Supreme Court." In such a society, "the people will have ceased to be their own rulers, having to that extent practically resigned their Government into the hands of that eminent tribunal."[15] Lincoln's professed judicial minimalism was hardly the stuff of Hamilton and Marshall, but rather of Madison. And it amounted to a bold challenge to the proper role of the Court in American political life. But what alternative did Lincoln have? If the Court were going to use its powers so irresponsibly, he was obliged to deny them future opportunities to do so.

Though it is an extreme case, *Dred Scott* highlights potential dangers of judicial review and the problems the political branches have when it is misused. Judicial review relies on little more than the justices' virtue to prevent them from reading their policy preferences into the law. Marshall possessed such greatness, which enabled him to build for the Court a reputation as a reliable steward of the constitutional order. But Taney used the powers bequeathed by Marshall to take one side over another in a fractious debate of extreme importance. That left the political branches with few options but to challenge the very legitimacy of Marshall's legacy, as Lincoln did in his inaugural address.

During the Civil War, the Court slunk into the background, chastened by the events that unfolded after *Dred Scott*. But within a generation, it was once more using the law to impose a particular worldview on the nation. This time, it was not the interests of the slaveholders, but those of industrial capitalists, which the Court would vigorously defend until its independence was again challenged by Franklin Roosevelt in 1937.

The United States entered the Industrial Revolution in the early decades of the 19th century, and by the time of the Civil War, the North had developed a fast-growing industrial sector. The war gave an incredible spur to this economic development, as the Union Army required all sorts of weapons and equipment to put down the rebellion. Rapid industrialization greatly increased the wealth of the nation, but it created a whole host of problems. Farmers were at the mercy of the railroad companies that owned the lines on which their crops were transported to market. Workers were forced to labor for long hours in dangerous conditions for little pay. Women and children were likewise drawn into the workforce. Meanwhile, the benefits of industrialization accumulated in the hands of a relatively few owners of capital. To many, industrialization seemed inconsistent with the basic principles of the republic. All individuals may have been born equal, but industrial capital had transformed some into masters of others.

In response, Americans increasingly agitated for government action to protect the welfare of workers and reduce the power of the rich. It was against this public clamor that the Court crafted for itself a new role. It staked a claim on behalf of the capitalists, arguing that the Constitution's protections for property rights required a laissez-faire approach to economic regulation. What is especially remarkable is how the Court went about this. The 14th Amendment, enacted after the Civil War, prevented the states from depriving "any person of life, liberty, or property, without due process of law."[16] Originally meant to protect the civil liberties of the freedmen, the Court reimagined it to protect business interests from any regulations that the Court found too burdensome.

How could this have happened again? Madison once more provides the answer—factionalism. After the Civil War, Democrats and Republicans became increasingly dependent on wealthy businessmen to finance their electoral campaigns. Consequently, both parties were responsive to the interests of capital and stocked the Courts with men who had once been corporate attorneys. These new justices instinctively considered any challenges to laissez-faire as a gateway to socialism. And since the power of judicial review placed the Court mostly outside the political process, the only check on it was the justices' prudence.

To be sure, the Court was usually strategic in defense of laissez-faire. It would lay down sweeping doctrines that seemingly prevented any limitations on capital, and then a few years later, it would discover a loophole or an exception. The rhyme or reason is tough to discover on a case-by-case basis, but in totality, the Court emerged as a kind of national super legislature. Any regulations—be they federal, state, or local—were not secure until the Court gave it the imprimatur of "due process." The aggregate statistics are remarkable. The Marshall Court (1801–35) struck down one federal law and 18 state laws. But the Melville Fuller Court (1889–1910) struck down 14 federal laws and 73 state laws, the Edward White Court (1910–21) struck down nine federal laws and 107 laws, and the William Howard Taft Court (1921–30) struck down 12 federal laws and 131 state laws.

After the Great Depression struck in 1929, the federal and state governments responded with evermore business regulations and greater social welfare protections. In response, the Court threw its previous caution to the wind. In the early 1930s, a majority of five conservative justices struck down one piece of progressive legislation after another. President Roosevelt, elected in 1932 to deal with the Depression, grew extremely frustrated, as the Court tore up much of his New Deal agenda. After his landslide victory in 1936, the president decided to act. By his reckoning, the people had given the New Deal a stamp of approval, and if the Court continued to obstruct it, then he would overhaul the Court. In 1937, he proposed expanding the size of the Court to overwhelm the votes of the conservatives with new, liberal justices. Like Lincoln before him, FDR rejected the ultimate authority of the Court to rule over the political branches, if it meant defeat of his policy initiatives.

Sure enough, the Court backed down. In 1937, Justice Owen Roberts, a member of the conservative bloc, switched his allegiance and supported progressive laws henceforth. This not only marked the triumph of the New Deal but also signaled a broader retreat by the Court on matters of regulation. It would be decades before the Court again challenged the scope of federal power. The subsequent Supreme Courts of Chief Justices Harlan Stone and Fred Vinson were relatively quiet, as the judiciary began to capitulate more regularly to the political branches.

Yet this deference would not last long. In due course, the old corporate attorneys were replaced with New Deal liberals who coalesced under the bold leadership of Chief Justice Earl Warren, ironically an appointee of the center-right Republican Dwight D. Eisenhower. Between 1953 and 1969, the liberal Warren Court struck down an astonishing number of laws, 23 on the federal level and 150 on the state level. Its interest was not so much in economics, but culture—in particular, the intersection of individual liberty and state action. The Warren Court's greatest accomplishment was to make good on the promise of racial equality under the law, first made with the Civil War amendments. In *Brown v. Board of Education* (1953), the Court overturned the old doctrine that allowed segregation in public facilities so long as they were nominally equal. The Court also upheld the constitutionality of the Civil Rights Act of 1964 and the Voting Rights Act of 1965.

Yet it did much more than this. From the late 1950s into the 1960s, the Court acted aggressively on behalf of civil liberties by embracing the doctrine of "incorporation." First articulated in the early 20th century, this idea held that the 14th Amendment incorporated the Bill of Rights into state constitutions, subjecting state actions against individual rights to judicial review. The Warren Court's rights revolution of the 1960s dramatically broadened the scope of free speech, prohibited prayer in public schools, expanded the rights of the accused, and limited the imposition of the death penalty. The Court even promulgated a "right to privacy," which, though not explicit in the Constitution, nevertheless was said to exist by implication in the Bill of Rights.

Liberals cheered these developments, as a Court acting on the right side of history, but the Court was once again picking sides in broader national disputes that, under the logic of Madisonian constitutionalism, should have been resolved through the political process. What secular liberals saw as the advocacy of core liberties, conservatives and Christians viewed as the Court protecting pornographers at the expense of common decency, secularism at the expense of traditional values, criminals at the expense of public order, and the sexual revolution at the expense of the traditional family. Conservatives were not wrong to see the Court as favoring one side of the cultural divide, despite its posture as a neutral arbiter of the law. Once more, the Court had become a kind of super legislature. No law—federal or state—that dealt even indirectly with the justices' preferred reading of the Bill of Rights was safe until the Court gave its assent.

Once again, the actions of the Court prompted a backlash. Richard Nixon won the presidency in 1968 in part on a pledge to rein in the Court. He met with limited success, for it was under his watch that in 1973 the Court issued *Roe v. Wade*. Written by Harry Blackmun, a Nixon appointee, *Roe* extended the right to privacy to include a right to abortion. Once more, liberals cheered. But many Christians found this deeply immoral and indeed offensive—that a Constitution dedicated to the protection of life could allow what they viewed as the murder of innocent children. The Warren Berger Court (1969–86) would dial down the brashness of Warren-era liberalism, but it still struck down 30 federal laws and 193 state laws, the latter of which is still a record.

In response, conservatives began to organize. Bit by bit, Republican presidents would make good on promises to their voters to replace liberals with conservatives who would reorient the Court. By the late 1980s, a moderately conservative Court was in place, and today the Court is more conservative than it has been at any point since the 1930s. As the current John Roberts Court pursues a conservative agenda, it is now liberals pointing out that the judiciary's views represent but a faction of society. Like the conservatives of the 1960s and 1970s, today's liberals are not wrong. The current Court has again carved out for itself the role as a kind of super legislature, striking down all manner of rules that do not comport with the justices' particular understanding of the Constitution.

* * * *

Judicial review as a policymaking project is a consequence of the gaps in the Constitution. The framers did not establish any formal ways to resolve disputes between the branches about the nature of the Constitution. Though Madison's idea of a Council of Revision was rejected, he still argued in *Federalist* 51 that something like it existed by implication. Each branch develops its own understanding of the Constitution, and the matter is settled through a political process whose purpose is to generate consensus. But, thanks to the work of Marshall, Hamilton's idea of judicial review triumphed. Over time, the Supreme Court acquired sweeping authority over the meaning of the Constitution and can now use its power of interpretations to set public policy.

There is a great historical irony here. The Court's power as a de facto lawmaking body stems in part through its power to interpret the Bill of Rights. Yet the Bill of Rights was not included in the original Constitution. Hamilton argued in *Federalist* 87 that a bill of rights was "not only unnecessary . . . but would even be dangerous."[17] It emerged as a compromise with Anti-Federalist critics of the Constitution, who thought it necessary for a formal enumeration of American rights. It was these very same critics who warned about the potential dangers of the Court. Thus, the Court acquired the expansive authority the Anti-Federalists warned about thanks in part to the demands of the Anti-Federalists themselves!

The political branches—the president, the House, and the Senate—have recourses against adverse Court decisions, but all of them are costly. They can amend the Constitution to reflect public values, as they did with the 16th Amendment, which legalized the income tax. But amendments take a long time to enact and require supermajorities within Congress and among the state legislatures. They can challenge the legitimacy of the Court, as both Lincoln and Roosevelt did, ignoring its rulings or threatening to redesign it altogether. But attacking the Court's legitimacy endangers the rule of law itself. They can restrict its appellate jurisdiction, but that requires the coordination of the political branches to pass a law. They can play a "long game," taking advantage of vacancies on the Court to shift its rulings, as the conservative movement has done in the past 50 years. While this respects the position of the Court in public life, it is a multigenerational project.

None of these solutions is consistent with the consensus-building nature of our political branches, which are rarely empowered to act on their own. Judicial review encourages the Court to act by itself, for it imposes heavy costs on the political branches to reject its rulings. That is exactly the opposite of Madison's vision in *Federalist* 51, where policymaking happens through the coordination of the branches. As Chief Justice Charles Evans Hughes put it, "We are under a Constitution, but the Constitution is what the judges say it is."[18]

It would be wonderful if the judiciary embodied the Hamiltonian ideal of a natural aristocracy. Often, it has. Marshall's tenure was a triumph, and the Warren Court's *Brown v. Board of Education* (1953) finally began the process of making good the promise of racial equality. Moreover, the overwhelming majority of the Court's docket involves disputes that do not entangle the judiciary with questions that properly belong to the political branches. The Court usually acts as the neutral arbiter it was intended to be.

But history has also been replete with moments of a factional court, using the power of judicial review to effectively write laws that impose its values on the rest of us. In those cases, the Court usually reflects the prejudices of the legal profession, whatever those may be at the time.

Before the Civil War, it embodied the motives of the slaveholding South. Afterward, the justices' backgrounds were in business, so the Court was pro-business. In the mid-20th century, justices tended to be New Dealers and sought to impose a sweeping vision of national liberalism. Today, the Court reflects the views of the conservative movement that has fought so hard to reshape it.

The constitutional process by which the political branches enact laws is supposed to reflect all the major interests of society while keeping any from being hegemonic. But factions can and have taken control of the Court and under the guise of interpreting the Constitution have rewritten it, privileging one set of values over others. While we today are prone to take judicial review as a given, such a sweeping of this power is fundamentally contrary to the constitutional vision of consensus-building.

9

Constitutional Virtue

The Constitution is an old system of government, which inspires in many conservatives an immediate sense of reverence and in progressives a feeling of repugnance. Its age makes it either worthy of esteem or outdated, depending on one's politics. But what I have tried to do in this book is move beyond these ideological dispositions and articulate the underlying philosophy of the Constitution. The framers adopted a sensible standard for lawmaking in a republic—the attainment of consensus— and put together a system that does a reasonably good job of achieving it. And while consensus certainly has its downsides, it is, I think, a necessary standard for a country as large and diverse as ours.

This creates a framework for considering how to improve our system. The Renaissance political theorist Niccolò Machiavelli recognized the inevitable necessity of reforming governments. In his *Discourses on Livy*, he praised states that "make frequent renovations possible," so that they can be led "back to their origins." For Machiavelli, it was at their starting points that "religious institutions, republics and kingdoms have in all cases some good in them, to which their early reputation and progress is due." But this "goodness is corrupted" over time, and "a body must of necessity die unless something happens which brings it up to the mark." Reform requires a political society to "return to its original principles."[1] Following Machiavelli, we should not merely admit the potential utility of reforms; we should consider them necessary. Governments naturally become corrupted over time and require an active, continuous effort to return them to the original idea that established them. And that idea was consensus.

Do proposed reforms make it easier for the country to generate consensus? If so, they are worthy of consideration. If not, then they are not. Several changes strike me as particularly useful in this regard. First, the House of Representatives should be expanded. Today's House district represents approximately three-quarters of a million people, larger than any state when the Constitution was ratified. It is not possible for a single person to represent fully such a large population, which means that the complete diversity of the people of the United States is not actually accounted for in the House. Consensus requires that all voices be heard, and the House no longer does that. The British House of Commons has over 500 seats, and the German Bundestag right now has more than 700. Surely, the American House can grow beyond 435 members, which has been set by law for a century and is now grossly outdated.

Expanding the size of the House would have the added advantage of decreasing the chances of "minority presidents," or those who win a majority in the Electoral College but lose the popular vote. From a strictly legal standpoint, the popular vote has no meaning, but from a philosophical standpoint, it is important. The democratic principle of majority rule is not a sufficient condition for governance in our system, but it should be necessary. It challenges this core principle of self-government to have a president who is not the first choice of the people. This has happened twice in the past quarter century: in 2000 when George W. Bush won a narrow Electoral College victory despite narrowly losing the popular vote and in 2016 when Donald Trump won the Electoral College despite winning nearly three million fewer votes than Hillary Clinton. Because electors to the Electoral College are apportioned based in part on House seats, expanding the House will benefit larger states primarily, especially California, where Al Gore and Clinton's "spare" votes were located.

Another way to reduce the chances of a minority presidency would be to encourage states to apportion electors proportionally, based on the results of the statewide vote. Right now, all states except Maine and Nebraska apportion their votes winner takes all, meaning that a candidate who wins a state by just one vote gets all their electors. Just as with the size of the House, the Constitution does not require this, and indeed in the early years of the republic, many states apportioned their electors proportionally. Returning to this would help sync the popular and electoral vote outcomes, which would be consistent with the principle of majority rule.

Additionally, reformers should turn their attention to the political parties, which have been allowed to develop with little to no consideration about the benefits they provide to our system. As noted in Chapter 7, we would be wise to heed the counsel of Martin Van Buren when it comes to parties—"to recognize their necessity, to give them the credit they deserve, and to devote ourselves to improve and to elevate the principles and objects of our own and to support it ingenuously and faithfully."[2] Most people would agree that parties are not doing a good job selecting the best candidates for public office, which is one of their core functions. They can and should be fixed so that they elevate the best among us, not the worst—as they so often seem to do.

What about the elaborate network of executive departments and agencies, commonly known as the bureaucracy? The bureaucracy is intended to implement the law dispassionately, relying on public administrators' policy expertise to do what Congress wishes as efficiently as possible. But over the years, Congress has effectively granted all kinds of policymaking power to the executive branch—and by extension the bureaucracy. Sometimes, sensitive policy matters, such as the setting of interest rates by the Federal Reserve, are so delicate that they cannot be left up to politics. But the executive branch has great leeway to make determinations about issues such as health care, abortion, immigration, and tariffs—all of which are best handled by building broad coalitions. The place that happens is Congress, which should seek to retrieve much of the authority it has dispersed over the generations.

But perhaps institutional reforms are akin to the tail wagging the dog. If we are unhappy about the state of our politics—which in all likelihood most readers are—perhaps we should consider that the problems with our institutions are but the symptoms of an underlying illness. Of course, we can and should try to improve them, but maybe the fault lies in ourselves. Do we as a people possess the correct virtues necessary for the democratic republic built by the framers? Do we even know what those virtues are? Maybe that which needs to be brought back to its origins, as Machiavelli put it, is we the people.

* * * *

It may seem strange to talk of civic virtue when discussing the United States Constitution. After all, delegates to the Constitutional Convention built it specifically to protect the republic in the decided absence of virtue. The people at large were always to be doubted. As James Madison put it in *Federalist* 55, "Had every Athenian citizen been a Socrates; every Athenian assembly would still have been a mob."[3] And while it is possible to empower individuals of wisdom and virtue, these "enlightened states-men," as Madison warned in *Federalist* 10, "will not always be at the helm."⁴ The Constitution is not premised on those of superior virtue pulling the levers of power, but rather on stopping decidedly average people from abusing their authority.

Moreover, the Constitution flatly prohibits the government from improving morals, and in this regard, it was ahead of its time. Western civ-ilization had long viewed religion as a bulwark of civic virtue and thus wor-thy of state support. It tempered selfish motives, encouraged obedience to the ruling authority, and inspired people to sacrifice themselves for the greater good. Most of Christendom had therefore joined the church and the state into a kind of symbiotic union, in which the one supported the other. Some within the Revolutionary generation of America still believed in the necessity of linking the secular and spiritual authority. In 1784, for instance, Patrick Henry proposed a bill that would have the government of Virginia subsidize all Christian churches, arguing that it would culti-vate good morals within the citizenry. But the tide in America was turn-ing against this idea, and the First Amendment, by separating church and state, decreed that statecraft was to be separate from soul craft.

Thus, the Constitution might seem to suggest that virtue is irrelevant. It can come across as a kind of machine, in which the inputs do not matter. People can be as selfish and shortsighted as they like. Their preferences will be balanced and checked within the institutions of government, ensur-ing that policy outputs will be for the good of the whole community.

But the truth is more complicated. The framers believed that goodness was often in short supply, and they certainly were convinced that the gov-ernment could not make people good. Neither proposition is the same as the notion that virtue is irrelevant. If a mob of Socrates is still a mob, incapable of spontaneously producing justice and needing sound govern-ing institutions to produce justice, no set of governing institutions can restrain a mob of Hitlers from seeking injustice. As Madison put it during the ratification debates in Virginia,

> Is there no virtue among us? If there be not, we are in a wretched situation. No theoretical checks—no form of government can render us secure. To suppose that any form of government will

secure liberty or happiness without any virtue in the people, is a chimerical idea.[5]

So the people have to have a basic level of decency for any free government to be sustained.

And the more virtuous the people are, the more the Constitution will empower the government to act. The founding charter presents the people with a kind of bargain: Find common ground, and the government will act; refuse to find it, and the government will be inert. The choice is up to the people. They can be obstreperous, stubbornly clinging to their own rectitude and refusing to acknowledge the legitimacy of other points of view. On the other hand, they can be ecumenical, granting the benefit of the doubt to those who disagree with them, and they can find points of commonality. The Constitution favors the latter over the former. Those who approach politics as a give-and-take process among competing interests are more likely to discover policy breakthroughs, while those who see it as a winner-takes-all battle of good versus evil are more likely to be disappointed.

Thus, even though the Constitution does not create institutions to reform the morals of the people, it still privileges a vision of politics that encourages us to overcome our all-too-human flaws. We are too prone to place our own interests above others in the community. We cannot appreciate the limits to our own understanding and thus mistake our own preferences for the true good. The Constitution is designed to limit the dangers that these frailties create, but when we overcome these natural vices, the more latitude we have for action. The Constitution is not merely about stopping factionalism; it creates a framework of government to help us discover our common interests.

The Constitution does not mandate that we see politics this way. If we are committed to the destruction of our political opponents, it is not going to reform our views. It will not cleanse our souls. It will merely thwart us in our selfish desires. On the other hand, if we are willing to acknowledge that each of us is merely part of a faction, and that we must work together, the Constitution creates a political forum for us to find that common ground and govern accordingly.

We can gain a stronger appreciation of this choice by comparing the ideology of politics today, with its roots in the fights of the 20th century, to the politics of the early 19th century. The Constitution was basically the same then as it is now. One of the major differences is how the people conceive of politics. Today, we see it as a fraught battle between good and evil, but in the Jeffersonian Era, it was more the forum where disputes could be resolved.

* * * *

Unfortunately, for all the good that they can do in our constitutional system, the parties often subvert civic virtue. Partisanship, in its extreme forms, can become a vicious factionalism—an "us versus them" mentality that brooks no compromise. Parties are useful for framing elections as contests not merely over candidates but political agendas, thus helping electoral judgments be more considered. Yet in their quest for electoral victory, they can induce a frenzied hatred of the political opposition—casting politics not as a competition between legitimate views of the public good but as a battle of right versus wrong.

When the parties have whipped up their supporters into such a delirious state, the political opportunities for meaningful compromise diminish. Elected officials dare not strike out for common ground with the opposition, lest they be punished by the strong partisans back home who form the backbone of their coalition. Without a spirit for compromise, the government grinds to a virtual halt, problems remain unresolved, and confidence in public institutions collapses—exactly what we have seen in the present age.

If you go by the rhetoric of the two parties today, politics is like a holy crusade. Politicians frequently invoke martial metaphors: One side pledges to "take back the White House" and another to "retake the House," as if either is territory that has been lost to the bad guys. Barack Obama, who initially ran as a candidate who would transcend this sort of politics, inadvertently captured its essence in 2010 when he encouraged Hispanic voters "to punish our enemies and . . . reward our friends."[6] In 2012, Mitt Romney told a group of Republican donors that 47 percent of the country is "dependent upon government, who believe that they are victims" and that his job as a candidate was "not to worry" about them.[7] Donald Trump's "Make America Great Again" slogan became a kind of martial anthem among his followers, with the implication that his political opposition had destroyed

America. Hillary Clinton denounced a large portion of the country as belonging to a "basket of deplorables."[8] Joe Biden has also castigated his Republican opponents as needing to have an "epiphany" that would break their opposition.[9]

Framing politics as a winner-takes-all fight between good and evil is hardly a new phenomenon. Perhaps its greatest expression came from Theodore Roosevelt. In 1912, Roosevelt challenged his one-time friend and political supporter, William Howard Taft, for the Republican presidential nomination. When Roosevelt lost, he and his supporters formed their own Progressive Party, which nominated him as its candidate. In his speech to the delegates, Roosevelt thundered:

> Surely there never was a fight better worth making than the one in which we are engaged. It little matters what befalls any one of us who for the time being stand in the forefront of the battle. I hope we shall win, and I believe that if we can wake the people to what the fight really means we shall win. But, win or lose, we shall not falter. Whatever fate may at the moment overtake any of us, the movement itself will not stop. Our cause is based on the eternal principles of righteousness; and even though we who now lead may for the time fail, in the end the cause itself shall triumph. Six weeks ago, here in Chicago, I spoke to the honest representatives of a Convention which was not dominated by honest men; a Convention wherein sat, alas! a majority of men who, with sneering indifference to every principle of right, so acted as to bring to a shameful end a party which had been founded over half a century ago by men in whose souls burned the fire of lofty endeavor. Now to you men, who, in your turn, have come together to spend and be spent in the endless crusade against wrong, to you who face the future resolute and confident, to you who strive in a spirit of brotherhood for the betterment of our Nation, to you who gird yourselves for this great new fight in the never-ending warfare for the good of humankind, I say in closing what in that speech I said in closing: We stand at Armageddon, and we battle for the Lord.[10]

Roosevelt has been remembered as one of America's great presidents, and rightly so. He was actually an adroit compromiser during his tenure (1901–09), finding ways to advance progressive policies within a Republican Party that still was predominantly conservative. This speech is not the measure of his legacy. Yet it nevertheless anticipates many of the vices of the present age.

Roosevelt explicitly equated his personal quest for the presidency with the "the eternal principles of righteousness." Politicians routinely do that today as well, warning voters that the very issue of national survival is on the ballot. He suggested that those who opposed his efforts to take the Republican nomination from Taft were operating in bad faith, exhibiting "sneering indifference to every principle of right." Again, politicians do that all the time today. Those who disagree are rarely, if ever, given the benefit of the doubt. Indeed, it is not even a question about whether they are wrong. They are knowingly, stubbornly, indifferently blind to the truth. And when the stakes are so high, many politicians join Roosevelt in analogizing their quest for political office into a holy crusade: "We stand at Armageddon, and we battle for the Lord."

Roosevelt's speech was meant to rally his deeply frustrated political supporters, and rhetoric in such circumstances can be fiery. The problem is that this rhetoric has now become the norm, rather than the exception. It is how, in the ordinary course of politics, the two political factions see each other today. Conservatives and liberals, Republicans and Democrats, conceive each other as totally, irredeemably corrupted. The two sides fight over everything, large and small, from major problems to utter trivialities. To borrow a phrase from Madison's *Federalist* 10, "where no substantial occasion presents itself," they will fight tooth and nail over "the most frivolous and fanciful distinctions."[11]

The mutual hatred between the left and the right leaves little political space for compromise. Fundamentally, they do not wish to compromise; they want to destroy each other. They hope that each election will be the final triumph of their side over the opposition, the victory of the forces of good over the forces of evil. So it is little wonder that our government has been riddled by gridlock. The left and right wish to be hegemonic, but the Constitution is designed to prevent factional hegemons from emerging in our country. If the two sides enter the government not with a spirit of compromise but a spirit of destruction, they should expect to be blocked at virtually every turn—which is precisely what has happened.

The problem is not so much that most Americans feel this way. Polling demonstrates that the broad middle of the country still prefers compromise between the parties. The problem has more to do with the fraction of hyper-partisan citizens who are most engaged in the process. They exercise outsized influence in our politics, in at least three ways.

First, they are most likely to watch cable news, and the corporations that own these outlets have an incentive to tailor their coverage to their prejudices, thus influencing the national discourse. Second, hyper-ideologues make up the base of small-dollar donors, whose aggregate contributions can direct vast sums of money, incentivizing politicians to cater to them. Third, they are more likely to vote in low-turnout primary elections, giving them extra power in determining the range of options in the general election. This can be a major problem in the House of Representatives. In safely Republican or safely Democratic districts, the winner of the primary is all but guaranteed a victory in the general election, and the result is a more polarized Congress.

And so, even as most Americans remain pragmatic and amenable to compromise, the political process looks closer to Roosevelt's vision of 1912. The extent to which Congress reflects the public views is distorted by the outsized influence of these ideologues. Despite widespread public dissatisfaction, politics becomes about the elevation of an ideology—or a single view of the good life above the others—instead of the recognition of the need for reconciliation among factions with different views.

It might come as a surprise to contemporary Americans, but politics has not always been this way. There have been periods in our country when big disagreements between the parties gave way to compromise and ultimately national reconciliation. The most significant was spearheaded by two of the most important men of the American founding— Thomas Jefferson and Madison—whose political moderation following their ascendancy to power in 1801 led eventually to the temporary collapse of the two-party system altogether, for the grounds of conflict simply evaporated. While it is unreasonable to expect a repeat of such a unique moment in American history, it nevertheless is worth thinking about how the Republicans managed to bind the wounds created during the fractious decade of the 1790s, for there may be something for us to learn for today's strife.

* * * *

The politics of the 1790s were ugly, as the country split over domestic and foreign affairs. Alexander Hamilton's financial program involved questions of not only finance but also how republican government was to function. The Republicans thought the Federalist vision too elite and insufficiently democratic. Nasty as this division was, it was made worse by the return of war between Britain and France, which broke out after the execution of King Louis XVI in January 1793. President George Washington endeavored to maintain a neutral ground between the combatants, but it was not easy. The Federalists, sensitive to the importance of commerce, supported the British, America's number one trading partner. The Republicans, drawn to the cause of French liberty, were partial to the new revolutionary government of France. Both sides accused the other of conspiring with a foreign power to subvert American interests. Fearful of the perceived radicalism and foreign influence of the Republicans, the Federalist-dominated Congress enacted the Sedition Act of 1798, which made it a crime to defame the government.

The year 1800 was the culmination of this partisan clash. Jefferson triumphed over John Adams for the presidency, and the Republicans won a large majority in Congress. The new president could have gone measure for measure against the Federalists and stuck them with a version of the same Sedition Act that had been imposed on the Republicans. However, in an often-overlooked gesture of national reconciliation, he purposefully turned down the political rhetoric. In his first inaugural address, Jefferson urged calm:

> We have called by different names brethren of the same principle. We are all republicans: we are all federalists. If there be any among us who would wish to dissolve this Union, or to change its republican form, let them stand undisturbed as monuments of the safety with which error of opinion may be tolerated, where reason is left free to combat it.[12]

The inauguration of 1801 has been celebrated as the first peaceful transfer of power—not just because Adams allowed Jefferson to take over but because Jefferson denounced any proscriptions of his Federalist opponents.

This was not mere rhetoric from Jefferson. While later presidents would usually purge their opponents from government offices, Jefferson generally allowed Federalists to remain. His administration also kept in place Hamilton's financial system and pursued broadly popular policies such as the Louisiana Purchase. In 1804, the Republicans were rewarded when Jefferson won all of Federalist New England except Connecticut. And in 1808, Sen. John Quincy Adams of Massachusetts—son of President John Adams—switched from the Federalist Party to the Republican Party, to which he would be committed for the next 20 years.

Republican foreign policy proved unpopular, however, after Britain and France returned to war in 1803. America was once more caught in the middle, and as an alternative to war, the Jefferson administration adopted a trade embargo in 1807. The Republicans hoped that the lack of American foodstuffs would force the European powers to treat America as a neutral party in the war, but it backfired. Instead, it wrecked the American economy, dealing a particularly heavy blow to New England, which depended heavily on trade between the United States and Europe. Madison succeeded Jefferson as president in 1809 and, after three years of failed efforts to gain British respect for American neutrality, asked for a declaration of war in June 1812. The war was staunchly opposed in New England, which refused to back the effort by supplying either loans to the government or troops for the militia.

Republican forbearance was still evident, however. The War of 1812 was generally popular, with pockets of extreme opposition, making it similar on the domestic front to the Civil War and World War I. But whereas Abraham Lincoln and Woodrow Wilson took steps to stifle dissent, Madison demurred. When Federalist opponents met at the Hartford Convention, where separation from the Union was discussed, Madison allowed it. That places him in stark contrast to other wartime presidents, especially Wilson, under whose administration socialist Eugene V. Debs, one of his opponents in the 1912 election, was actually jailed for speaking out against the war.

With the end of the war in the winter of 1814–15, the foreign policy crisis that had plagued the country for nearly a decade had passed, and the Republicans returned to building a broad domestic political coalition. The Republicans supported old Hamiltonian ideas such as a national bank and a protective tariff. But whereas Hamilton's original plans tended to favor eastern merchants, the Republicans redesigned these policies to broaden the scope of beneficiaries. Their tariffs helped farmers in the Midwest, and they opened branches of the Bank of the United States all throughout the nation, rather than just the big cities of the North. The Republicans also embraced internal improvements—roads, bridges, and canals—as a way to bind the country closer together. And they made crucial investments in the permanent military establishment, by improving the military academy at West Point and expanding the quartermaster department, which helped the country triumph in future conflicts.

These policies antagonized people at opposite ends of the policy spectrum. Die-hard Republicans, like John Randolph of Roanoke, believed that the party had abandoned its old orthodoxies. Federalists like Rufus King and Daniel Webster thought they did not go far enough. But still, the broad middle of the country was satisfied, and James Monroe, longtime friend of Jefferson and Madison, was elected overwhelmingly to the presidency in 1816. In 1820, he faced no opposition whatsoever, marking the high point of the "Era of Good Feelings."

Some Republicans, Monroe included, thought that party politics was gone for good. In a letter to Andrew Jackson from 1816, Monroe looked forward to a one-party future. He admitted "that the ancient republics were always divided into parties" and "the English government is maintained by a minister." But he thought the "cause of these divisions" was "certain defects of those governments" and not "in human nature." Thanks to the American Constitution, "we have happily avoided those defects in our system," and thus the existence of the Federalist Party was not "necessary to keep union and order in the Republican ranks."[13]

Alas, it was not to be. The Era of Good Feelings was fleeting. The issue of slavery would soon rend the country apart. The question of territorial expansion, and just how aggressive it should be, would also alienate New England from the South and West. And Andrew Jackson would ride a populist wave into the White House in 1828, creating new divisions within the country between those who thought he spoke for the people and those who, like his opponent Henry Clay, judged him a mere "military chieftain."[14]

Still, the period of Republican dominance—from 1801 to 1825—is a remarkable moment in American political history. It sits between two periods of notable divisiveness, the Federalist era of the 1790s and the age of Jackson from the 1820s into the 1840s. Plenty of issues could have continued to divide the country, but the "Virginia dynasty" of Jefferson, Madison, and Monroe took seriously the virtue of forbearance that Jefferson extolled in his first inaugural address. Though they had very much contributed to the nastiness of the 1790s, they genuinely believed that the bulk of the Federalist opposition could be won over through moderation and conciliation. They were right.

The Virginia dynasty not only won six straight elections, usually by overwhelming margins, but also remade American politics. They laid the foundations for a truly democratic republic, doing away with the high-toned, aristocratic model preferred by some Federalists. And after the War of 1812, they established the basic outlines of a pro-development American economic policy, which would endure for generations. That they did all this with widespread public support speaks to the potential of the politics of consensus.

* * * *

Party politics was probably bound to return in some form or another. The United States of the early 19th century was much more homogeneous than today. It was easier to find common ground, as fewer factional differences separated the people. And strong parties can be a good thing. They frame elections over the issues of the day, which enhances consensus by informing voters and making their judgments more considered.

The point is not to idealize the Jeffersonian era—nor to deny that Jefferson, Madison, and Monroe all contributed to the nastiness of the 1790s—but rather to draw lessons about how the people of that time, both average Americans and elites, viewed politics. They wanted political harmony, believed that common ground was possible, and found ways to make it a reality. They did not go measure for measure against their political opponents. They looked for avenues of reconciliation. They understood the difference between opinions and principles. They appreciated that a free-flowing discourse was essential to discovering shared interests. Our consensus-based institutions of government rewarded their efforts, as their reforms set the stage for American political and economic development for the 19th century.

The United States of the 21st century makes no such collective effort. Instead, Roosevelt's extraordinary rhetoric in 1912 has become ordinary for us. We declare all differences of opinion as not only differences of principle but signs of our opponents' evil. Politics has become like a religion—and a simplistic Manichaeism at that. This is true of our political elites, as this rhetoric comes from the top; and it is true of average Americans, many of whom ravenously feast on a steady diet of political hatred, through both social media and cable news.

This is no way to run a country—any country. But it certainly dooms us to failure under a consensus-based regime like the United States Constitution. If we want to rail against the evils of our opponents for nothing more than the sheer pleasure of the cathartic release, so be it. Nothing will get done while we spew our splenetic bile at one another. But if we actually want to solve problems in this country, we need to recognize that, under our system of government, working together is the only way to do that.

Conclusion

The past 100 years of world history have been a triumph for democracy, the likes of which is only believable in historical retrospect. It was not long ago that democracy seemed to be an also-ran in the contest of governing principles. Radicals on both the left and the right—the Soviets in Russia, the Nazis in Germany, and the Fascists in Italy—rejected the system outright. Great Britain, the innovator of many modern principles of democracy, denied the right of self-determination to the peoples under its imperial dominion. Likewise, France was democratic at home but authoritarian abroad. The United States still denied African Americans in the South the right to participate in the body politic.

But today, democracy is ascendant. Most of Europe has adopted democratic rule. The old European empires have collapsed, and many previous imperial possessions likewise are democratic. The system of government thrives among large swaths of the non-Western world—in not only India, Japan, and South Korea in Asia but also Brazil, Chile, and Colombia in South America. No doubt, some of these regimes are more democratic than others. And other nations remain stubbornly authoritarian—most notably, China, North Korea, and Russia, while large portions of Africa remain under the tyranny of dictatorship. But these are exceptions to the bigger story of democratic revolution. Particularly among Westerners, democracy has become the hegemonic ideology of governance. No alternative can make any serious bid for legitimacy.

Democracy has advantages that no other system of government can provide. It encourages mass participation in the affairs of state, which generates loyalty to the regime. In totalitarian systems, obedience usually requires a combination of fear and propaganda. Democracy also fits in snugly with the rights revolution that has overtaken the West; if individuals are truly meant to be autonomous, it stands to reason that they should also have the right to participate in public decisions that will affect them. Democracy also leverages the wisdom of crowds, in the same way that the free market successfully sets prices. Rather than relying exclusively on a handful of elites to determine what the public interest is and how to achieve it, democracy outsources many decisions to the people themselves. Individuals know their own circumstances best and so are collectively able to provide insight that central planners simply lack.

And yet, even as we acknowledge that democracy is the best system of government, we must remember that it is not an end in itself. It is but a means to an end. Government is meant to protect justice and promote the general welfare. That is what a republic is supposed to accomplish— hence the title question of the book. Democracy and republic are not interchangeable terms.

Still, they are related. Most of the American framers believed that democracy was a necessary condition of a republic. They rejected the idea that Great Britain was a truly free state, with its limited franchise and its power reserved to the king. And while they certainly admired the ingenious organization of power within the Roman Republic, it was far too aristocratic for American tastes. James Madison put it best in *Federalist* 39, when he argued that the government of any true republic must "be derived from the great body of the society." And while he believed that "persons administering it" could be "appointed, either directly or indirectly, by the people," no true republic could rely on "an inconsiderable" or "favored class" of the people.[1] Every office had to trace back to the people, either directly or indirectly, because the only way the government can rule on behalf of the public is if it reflects it.

While democracy is a necessary condition for a republic, it is not sufficient. It would be nice if the people would always rule with an eye toward justice and the common good, but all the evidence from the history of our nature demonstrates otherwise. The framers were well aware of the collapse of democratic Athens in the golden age of Greece. They also could look closer to home, at the way the states under the Articles of Confederation ignored the good of the nation and trampled on the rights of political minorities. And as Polybius advised, every system of government is liable to be corrupted; a democratic republic will collapse into a democratic tyranny.

The Americans sought to escape this fate through the Constitution. It relies on the principle of democracy as the foundation of the regime, but it structures popular sovereignty to prevent the republic from being corrupted into democratic tyranny. The people ultimately write the law in this country, but they do so under the constraints of consensus. Democratic majorities need to be large, broad, and considered to enact meaningful changes in our polity, for such coalitions are more likely to reflect the true interests of the community.

The framers' approach to the Constitution has an analogue in our legal system. Juries are a truly democratic form of governance. Their members are chosen at random from the population, just as the Athenians used to choose some officers by lot. Juries represent the people in any legal dispute, and they have complete sovereignty over the facts of the case. But they do not have carte blanche over the proceedings. Instead, what they are allowed to consider is determined by the rule of law, which enables them to render verdicts according to the principles of justice. The standard of consensus serves the same function in our politics as the law does in jury trials. It guides the people toward decisions that respect the rights of others and advances the interests of the community.

We see this at every step along the way in the Constitution's lawmaking process—which structures both popular sovereignty and the political combat among elites. Democratic representation helps refine public opinion, by hopefully elevating those individuals who can divine the true interests of their constituents. Bicameralism creates two distinct versions of the public mind, which must agree with one another for any law to be enacted—reducing the chances that an intemperate majority enacts bad laws or a clique of elites hijacks the lawmaking process. The House, by reflecting the United States in all its diversity, includes a multitude of factions, therefore reducing the chances that any one group dominates. The Senate, by representing the interests of the states, gives special voice to geographically distinct minorities. The president, as an officer elected by the whole people, has a final check on the legislative process to ensure that Congress keeps its eye on the big picture.

Admittedly, the sum total is a complicated system of government that often seems ramshackle and haphazard. But the pieces of the puzzle fit together meaningfully. The Constitution seeks to defend, as Madison put it at the Constitutional Convention, "[against] the inconveniencies of democracy" while remaining "consistent with the democratic form of [government]."[2] The people rule in our system, but by forcing them to achieve consensus, the Constitution increases the chances that their rule benefits society.

The system is not perfect. No system is. There are costs to consensus. It is inefficient, as bringing in a multitude of factions to the governing coalition can make the task of necessary legislation more costly and time-consuming than with simple majoritarianism. It is often slow to address problems before they become crises. It can perpetuate injustice, especially when those who are mistreated do not enjoy the rights of citizenship. While the parties can enhance the prospects of consensus by improving public judgments, they too often encourage extreme factionalism. While the Supreme Court can serve as a wise and neutral arbiter in disputes, it has also used the power of judicial review to act as a hegemonic faction, dividing the country and inhibiting the chances of consensus. And a system founded on consensus works best when the people embody a spirit of mutual respect and an earnest desire for true accommodation to one another—a virtue that is decidedly lacking nowadays.

Nevertheless, a country as large and diverse as ours, without any clear ethnic, religious, economic, or cultural signifier of "we the people," must be founded on the principle of consensus. That is what makes us so different from the democracies of Europe, many of which rely on more majoritarian mechanisms. America is not Sweden. Ours is a continent-spanning republic whose people defy any uniform classification. Loyalty to our regime can only be produced in one way—a broad-based conviction that meaningfully reflects each faction's own unique preferences and beliefs. That requires consensus. And while we might often find ourselves frustrated by the gridlock of day-to-day politics, our Constitution has created a framework by which an ever-growing number of people can peacefully live together.

In the final analysis of the Constitution, perhaps the inestimable Benjamin Franklin offered the best argument in its favor. There are many ways to criticize our system of government, just as anyone can find fault with anything if they look hard enough. But realistically, the Constitution, as Franklin put it, is a stunning achievement.

> I doubt . . . whether any other Convention we can obtain, may
> be able to make a better Constitution. For when you assemble a

number of men to have the advantage of their joint wisdom, you inevitably assemble with those men, all their prejudices, their passions, their errors of opinion, their local interests, and their selfish views. From such an assembly can a perfect production be expected? It therefore astonishes me, Sir, to find this system approaching so near to perfection as it does; and I think it will astonish our enemies, who are waiting with confidence to hear that our councils are confounded like those of the Builders of Babel; and that our States are on the point of separation, only to meet hereafter for the purpose of cutting one another's throats. Thus I consent, Sir, to this Constitution because I expect no better, and because I am not sure, that it is not the best.[3]

Judged against an ideal system that has never been and will never be, our system may seem a bit of a letdown. But in the real world, it remains a true marvel, a historic achievement, and a continued blessing for generations of citizens of the United States, a nation on the verge of its 250th year as a democratic republic.

Acknowledgments

This work would not have been possible without the assistance of many people, to whom I owe a great debt of gratitude. First and above all, I would like to express my gratitude to my wife, Lindsay. She was, as always, patient with me as I went through the ups and downs of putting this book together. She also provided incredibly useful feedback at the editing stage of this project. Whatever merits this work may possess, it was made better because of her.

Thanks to the American Enterprise Institute, which since 2019 has offered me an opportunity to think through issues like those discussed in this book. Indeed, the very idea of this book came from a series of reports I wrote for AEI titled "The Conservative Case for the Constitution." Thanks in particular to Yuval Levin and Nicole Penn of the Social, Cultural, and Constitutional Studies division; my research assistants John Roach and Max Markon; my editor Rachel Hershberger; and Claude Aubert and Jennifer Morretta of the Design team.

Thanks to Paul Kengor, Robert Rider, and Brenda Vinton of the Institute for Faith & Freedom at Grove City College for providing me with a forum over the years to develop many of the ideas that appear in these pages.

Thanks to Luke Thompson, the cohost of our *Constitutionally Speaking* podcast. Working with him over the past few years has enormously improved my understanding of the Constitution. He also helped me worked through several stickier points in the manuscript.

Thanks to Jaime Lockwood and Mary Barnes for the opportunity to teach at Portersville Christian School. Engaging high schoolers in social studies has been an enormous challenge but rewarding. It has helped me refine my ideas on history, politics, and philosophy in ways I never thought possible. Thanks as well to my students, for (mostly) paying attention while I prattled on endlessly about the genius of James Madison.

About the Author

Jay Cost is the Gerald R. Ford nonresident senior fellow at the American Enterprise Institute (AEI), where he focuses on political theory, Congress, and elections. He is also a visiting scholar at Grove City College and a contributing editor at the *Washington Examiner*. His previous books include *James Madison: America's First Politician* (Basic Books, 2021); *The Price of Greatness: Alexander Hamilton, James Madison, and the Creation of American Oligarchy* (Basic Books, 2018); and *A Republic No More: Big Government and the Rise of Political Corruption* (Encounter Books, 2015). He earned a PhD in political science from the University of Chicago and a BA in government and history from the University of Virginia.

Notes

Introduction

1. Greg Coleridge and Jessica Munger, "The U.S. Constitution Is Hopelessly Outdated. It's Time to Re-Envision It," Salon, December 10, 2020, https://www.salon.com/2020/12/10/the-us-constitution-is-hopelessly-outdated-its-time-to-re-envision-it.

2. Michael Klarman, "Foreword: The Degradation of American Democracy—and the Court," *Harvard Law Review* 134, no. 1 (November 2020), https://harvardlawreview.org/wp-content/uploads/2020/11/134-Harv.-L.-Rev.-1.pdf.

3. Sanford Levinson, "The Constitution *Is* the Crisis," *Atlantic*, October 1, 2019, https://www.theatlantic.com/ideas/archive/2019/10/the-constitution-is-the-crisis/598435.

4. James Fallows, "A Lucky Country, on Thin Ice," Breaking the News, June 20, 2022, https://fallows.substack.com/p/a-lucky-country-on-thin-ice.

5. Quoted in Jonathan Turley, "Georgetown Law Professor Rosa Brooks: The Problem Is the Constitution Which Enslaves Us," July 6, 2022, https://jonathanturley.org/2022/07/06/georgetown-law-professor-rosa-brooks-the-problem-is-the-constitution-which-enslaves-us.

6. Woodrow Wilson, "Responsible Government Under the Constitution," *Atlantic*, April 1886, https://www.theatlantic.com/magazine/archive/1886/04/responsible-government-under-the-constitution/519561.

7. Thomas Jefferson, letter to James Madison, September 6, 1789, Founders Online, https://founders.archives.gov/documents/Jefferson/01-15-02-0375-0003.

8. Paul Waldman, "This July 4, Let's Declare Our Independence from the Founding Fathers," *Washington Post*, July 4, 2022, https://www.washingtonpost.com/opinions/2022/07/04/july-4-declare-independence-founding-fathers.

9. Abraham Lincoln, "The Gettysburg Address," Abraham Lincoln Online, https://www.abrahamlincolnonline.org/lincoln/speeches/gettysburg.htm.

10. Turley, "Georgetown Law Professor Rosa Brooks."

Chapter 1. The Basics

1. Aristotle, *The Politics*, trans. Trevor J. Saunders and T. A. Sinclair (New York: Penguin Classics, 1981).

2. John Locke, *Second Treatise of Government*, ed. C. B. Macpherson (Indianapolis, IN: Hackett Publishing Company, 1980).

3. Edmund Burke, "Speech on Conciliation with the Colonies," in *The Founders' Constitution*, vol. 1, ed. Philip B. Kurland and Ralph Lerner (Chicago: University of Chicago, 1986), https://press-pubs.uchicago.edu/founders/documents/v1ch1s2.html.

4. Isaac Newton, *The Principia* (Amherst, NY: Prometheus Books, 1995).

5. Francis Bacon, *Novum Organum* (London: Forgotten Books, 2010).

6. Locke, *Second Treatise of Government*; and Montesquieu, *Spirit of the* Laws, ed. Anne M. Cohler, Basia C. Miller, and Harold S. Stone (Cambridge, UK: Cambridge University Press, 1989).

7. Adam Smith, *Wealth of Nations* (Amherst, NY: Prometheus Books, 1991).

8. See, for instance, Robert Bucholz, *A History of England from the Tudors to the Stuarts* (Chantilly, VA: Teaching Company, 2003), 19–23.

9. Carl Richard, *The Founders and the Classics: Greece, Rome and the American Enlightenment* (Cambridge, MA: Harvard University Press, 1995), 9.

10. Declaration of Independence (US 1776).

11. Montesquieu, *Spirit of the Laws*, 131.

12. Montesquieu, *Spirit of the Laws*.

13. National Archives, "Articles of Confederation," https://www.archives.gov/milestone-documents/articles-of-confederation.

14. Roland Emmerich, dir., *The Patriot* (Culver City, CA: Columbia Pictures, 2000).

15. Polybius, *The Histories*, vol. 2, ed. and trans., Evelyn Shirley Shuckburgh (Cambridge, UK: Cambridge University Press, 1889), 466.

16. Polybius, *The Histories*.

17. Polybius, *The Histories*, 467.

18. Max Farrand, ed., *The Records of the Federal Convention of 1787* (New Haven, CT: Yale University Press, 1966), 3:13–14.

19. Quoted in James Madison, *Notes of Debates in the Federal Convention of 1787* (Athens, OH: Ohio University Press, 1984), 659.

20. Drew DeSilver, "U.S. Population Keeps Growing, but House of Representatives Is Same Size as in Taft Era," Pew Research Center, May 31, 2018, https://www.pewresearch.org/fact-tank/2018/05/31/u-s-population-keeps-growing-but-house-of-representatives-is-same-size-as-in-taft-era.

21. Samuel Adams, "Samuel Adams to Richard Henry Lee," in *The Founders' Constitution*, vol. 1, ed. Philip B. Kurland and Ralph Lerner (Chicago: University of Chicago, 1986), https://press-pubs.uchicago.edu/founders/documents/v1ch8s20.html.

Chapter 2. A National Republic

1. James Madison, letter to George Washington, April 16, 1787, Founders Online, https://founders.archives.gov/documents/Madison/01-09-02-0208.

2. *Federalist*, no. 51 (James Madison).

3. US Const. pmbl.

4. Thomas Paine, *Selected Writings*, ed. Ian Shapiro and Jane E. Calvert (New Haven, CT: Yale University Press, 2014).

5. Paine, *Selected Writings*.

6. Paine, *Selected Writings*.

7. Quoted in Jay Cost, *A Republic No More: Big Government and the Rise of Political Corruption* (New York: Encounter Books, 2015), 140.

8. Cost, *A Republic No More*.

9. Cost, *A Republic No More*.

10. David Hume, *An Enquiry Concerning Human Understanding* (Oxford, UK: Oxford University Press, 2008), 184.

11. David Hume, *Political Essays*, ed. Knud Haakonssen (Cambridge, UK: Cambridge University Press, 1994), 20.

12. Bruce Gordon, *John Calvin's The Institutes of the Christian Religion* (Princeton, NJ: Princeton University Press, 2016).

13. Edmund Burke, *Revolutionary Writings*, ed. Iain Hampsher-Monk (Cambridge, UK: Cambridge University Press, 2014), 90.

14. Karl Popper, *Selections*, ed. David Miller (Princeton, NJ: Princeton University Press, 1985), 7.

15. F. A. Hayek, *The Road to Serfdom* (Chicago: University of Chicago Press, 1994), 66.

16. *Federalist*, no. 10 (James Madison).

17. James Madison, letter to George Washington, April 16, 1787, Founders Online, https://founders.archives.gov/documents/Madison/01-09-02-0208.

18. *Federalist*, no. 9 (Alexander Hamilton).

Chapter 3. Checks and Balances

1. *Federalist*, no. 10 (James Madison).

2. *Federalist*, no. 10 (Madison).

3. John F. Kennedy, *Profiles in Courage* (New York: Harper, 2003).

4. Max Farrand, ed., *The Records of the Federal Convention of 1787* (New Haven, CT: Yale University Press, 1996), 1:151.

5. *Federalist*, no. 62 (Madison).

6. Edmund Burke, "Speech to the Electors at Bristol, November 3, 1774," in *The Founders' Constitution*, vol. 1, ed. Philip B. Kurland and Ralph Lerner (Chicago: University of Chicago, 1986), https://press-pubs.uchicago.edu/founders/documents/v1ch13s7.html.

7. Polybius, *The Histories of Polybius*, vol. 2, ed. Evelyn S. Shuckburgh (Cambridge, UK: Cambridge University Press, 2012).

8. James Madison, "Term of the Senate, [26 June 1787]," Founders Online, https://founders.archives.gov/documents/Madison/01-10-02-0044.

9. Madison, "Term of the Senate, [26 June 1787]."

10. Brutus, "Brutus XVI," Teaching American History, https://teachingamericanhistory.org/document/brutus-xvi.

11. *Federalist*, no. 47 (James Madison).

12. *Federalist*, no. 48 (James Madison).

13. *Federalist*, no. 49 (James Madison).

14. *Federalist*, no. 51 (James Madison).

15. *Federalist*, no. 51 (Madison).

16. Polybius, *The Histories of Polybius*, vol. 1, ed. Evelyn S. Shuckburgh (Cambridge, UK: Cambridge University Press, 2012).

17. *Federalist*, no. 48 (Madison).

Chapter 4. The Lawmaking Process

1. Abraham Lincoln, "Gettysburg Address Delivered at Gettysburg Pa. Nov. 19th 1863," Library of Congress, https://www.loc.gov/resource/rbpe.24404500.

2. *Federalist*, no. 10 (James Madison).

3. *Federalist*, no. 10 (Madison).

4. *Federalist*, no. 10 (Madison).

5. James Madison, letter to George Washington, April 16, 1787, Founders Online, https://founders.archives.gov/documents/Madison/01-09-02-0208.

6. *Federalist*, no. 10 (Madison).

7. *Federalist*, no. 10 (Madison).

8. *Federalist*, no. 10 (Madison).

9. *Federalist*, no. 10 (Madison).

10. Max Farrand, ed., *The Records of the Federal Convention of 1787* (New Haven, CT: Yale University Press, 1996), 1:65.

11. Farrand, ed., *The Records of the Federal Convention of 1787*, 2:36.

12. *Federalist*, no. 62 (James Madison).

13. Farrand, ed., *The Records of the Federal Convention of 1787*, 1:4.

14. Farrand, ed., *The Records of the Federal Convention of 1787*, 1:167.

15. Farrand, ed., *The Records of the Federal Convention of 1787*, 1:450.

16. Farrand, ed., *The Records of the Federal Convention of 1787*, 1:179.

17. Farrand, ed., *The Records of the Federal Convention of 1787*, 1:324.

18. Farrand, ed., *The Records of the Federal Convention of 1787*, 1:37.

19. Farrand, ed., *The Records of the Federal Convention of 1787*, 2:81.

20. Farrand, ed., *The Records of the Federal Convention of 1787*, 1:320–21.

21. Farrand, ed., *The Records of the Federal Convention of 1787*, 1:492.

22. Farrand, ed., *The Records of the Federal Convention of 1787*, 1:483.

23. Farrand, ed., *The Records of the Federal Convention of 1787*, 1:489.

24. Farrand, ed., *The Records of the Federal Convention of 1787*, 1:486.

25. Farrand, ed., *The Records of the Federal Convention of 1787*, 1:463.

26. Farrand, ed., *The Records of the Federal Convention of 1787*, 1:357.

27. Farrand, ed., *The Records of the Federal Convention of 1787*, 1:466.

28. Farrand, ed., *The Records of the Federal Convention of 1787*, 1:486.

29. Farrand, ed., *The Records of the Federal Convention of 1787*, 1: 51.

30. Farrand, ed., *The Records of the Federal Convention of 1787*, 1:404–5.

31. Farrand, ed., *The Records of the Federal Convention of 1787*, 1:407.

32. Farrand, ed., *The Records of the Federal Convention of 1787*, 1:398.

33. Farrand, ed., *The Records of the Federal Convention of 1787*.

34. Farrand, ed., *The Records of the Federal Convention of 1787*, 1:445–46.

35. Farrand, ed., *The Records of the Federal Convention of 1787*, 1:532–33.

36. Farrand, ed., *The Records of the Federal Convention of 1787*, 1:2–3.

37. Farrand, ed., *The Records of the Federal Convention of 1787*, 1:167.

38. *Federalist*, no. 10 (Madison).

39. Harry Truman quoted in Harry S. Truman Library and Museum, "'The Buck Stops Here' Desk Sign," https://www.trumanlibrary.gov/education/trivia/buck-stops-here-sign.

40. Declaration of Independence (US 1776).

41. *Federalist*, no. 70 (Alexander Hamilton).

Chapter 5. The Necessity of Consensus

1. BBC, "EU Referendum: The Result in Maps and Charts," June 8, 2021, https://www.bbc.com/news/uk-politics-36616028.

2. *Federalist*, no. 10 (James Madison).

3. James Madison, "Spirit of Governments," February 18, 1792, Founders Online, https://founders.archives.gov/documents/Madison/01-14-02-0203.

4. Madison, "Spirit of Governments."

5. Madison, "Spirit of Governments."

6. Madison, "Spirit of Governments."

7. Madison, "Spirit of Governments."

8. Farrand, ed., *The Records of the Federal Convention of 1787*, 1:179.

Chapter 6. Dead-Hand Control?

1. Alexander Hamilton, letter to James A. Bayard, April 16–21, 1802, Founders Online, https://founders.archives.gov/documents/Hamilton/01-25-02-0321.

2. David Hume, "Hume on the Origin of Government," Online Library of Liberty, https://oll.libertyfund.org/page/hume-on-the-origin-of-government.

3. Hume, "Hume on the Origin of Government."

4. *Federalist*, no. 49 (James Madison).

5. US Const. art. I, § 8, cl. 3.

6. US Const. art. I, § 8, cl. 1.

7. US Const. art. I, § 8, cl. 18.

8. US Const. amend. XIV.

9. US Const. amend. VIII.

10. Nikole Hannah-Jones, "America Wasn't a Democracy Until Black Americans Made It One," *New York Times Magazine*, August 14, 2019, https://www.nytimes.com/interactive/2019/08/14/magazine/black-history-american-democracy.html.

11. Centinel, "Centinel III," November 8, 1787, Teaching American History, https://teachingamericanhistory.org/library/document/centinel-iii.

12. Max Farrand, ed., *The Records of the Federal Convention of 1787* (New Haven, CT: Yale University Press, 1966), 1:587.

13. Wilfred Codrington III, "The Electoral College's Racist Origins," *Atlantic*, November 17, 2019, https://www.theatlantic.com/ideas/archive/2019/11/electoral-college-racist-origins/601918.

14. Codrington, "The Electoral College's Racist Origins."

Chapter 7. The Parties

1. US Const. pmbl.

2. See John Aldrich, *Why Parties* (Chicago: University of Chicago Press, 1995).

3. See V. O. Key Jr., *Politics, Parties & Pressure Groups*, 5th ed. (New York: Thomas Crowell, 1964).

4. See Noble E. Cunningham, *The Jeffersonian Republicans: The Formation of Party Organization* (Chapel Hill, NC: University of North Carolina Press, 1957), 15–29; and Forrest McDonald, *The Presidency of Thomas Jefferson* (Lawrence, KS: University Press of Kansas, 1976), 34–35.

5. See Cunningham, *The Jeffersonian Republicans*, 347–55.

6. See Edward Larson, *A Magnificent Catastrophe: The Tumultuous Election of 1800, America's First Presidential Campaign* (New York: Free Press, 2008), 87–111.

7. Quoted in Donald Henderson Stewart, *The Opposition Press of the Federalist Period* (Albany, NY: State University of New York Press, 1969), 11.

8. See John Zvesper, "The Madisonian Systems," *Western Political Quarterly* 37, no. 2 (1984): 236–56.

9. See Lance Banning, *The Sacred Fire of Liberty: James Madison and the Founding of the Federal Republic* (Ithaca, NY: Cornell University Press, 1997), 3.

10. *Federalist*, no. 10 (James Madison).

11. James Madison, "Popular Election of the First Branch of the Legislature, [6 June] 1787," Founders Online, http://founders.archives.gov/documents/Madison/01-10-02-0021.

12. *Federalist*, no. 10 (Madison).

13. See Jay Cost, *The Price of Greatness: James Madison, Alexander Hamilton and the Creation of American Oligarchy* (New York: Basic Books, 2018), 35–53.

14. See Whitney K. Bates, "Northern Speculators and Southern State Debts: 1790," *William and Mary Quarterly* 19, no. 1 (1962): 30–48.

15. See Cost, *The Price of Greatness*, 53–102.

16. In 1792, he wrote to Henry "Lighthorse Harry" Lee that if Alexander Hamilton's broad understanding of "general welfare" was adopted, the constitutional "parchment had better be thrown into the fire at once." James Madison, letter to Henry Lee, January 1, 1792, Founders Online, http://founders.archives.gov/documents/Madison/01-14-02-0158.

17. James Madison, "The Bank Bill," Founders Online, February 8, 1791, http://founders.archives.gov/documents/Madison/01-13-02-0284.

18. *Federalist*, no. 10 (Madison).

19. James Madison, letter to Thomas Jefferson, August 8, 1791, Founders Online, http://founders.archives.gov/documents/Madison/01-14-02-0062.

20. James Madison, "A Candid State of Parties," Founders Online, September 22, 1792, http://founders.archives.gov/documents/Madison/01-14-02-0334.

21. James Madison, "The Union. Who Are Its Real Friends?," Founders Online, March 31, 1792, http://founders.archives.gov/documents/Madison/01-14-02-0245.

22. James Madison, "Parties," Founders Online, January 23, 1792, http://founders.archives.gov/documents/Madison/01-14-02-0176.

23. Madison, "A Candid State of Parties."

24. James Madison, "Consolidation," Founders Online, December 3, 1791, http://founders.archives.gov/documents/Madison/01-14-02-0122.

25. Madison, "The Union."

26. James Madison, "Spirit of Governments," Founders Online, February 18, 1792, http://founders.archives.gov/documents/Madison/01-14-02-0203.

27. Madison, "The Union."

28. Madison, "A Candid State of Parties."

29. Madison, "Consolidation."

30. Madison, "Consolidation."

31. James Madison, "Government," Founders Online, December 31, 1791, http://founders.archives.gov/documents/Madison/01-14-02-0157.

32. James Madison, "Charters," Founders Online, January 18, 1792, http://founders.archives.gov/documents/Madison/01-14-02-0172.

33. Madison, "Consolidation."

34. Madison, "Consolidation."

35. James Madison, "For the *National Gazette*," Founders Online, 4 February 1792," https://founders.archives.gov/documents/Madison/01-14-02-0190.

36. Madison, "Parties."

37. Madison, "A Candid State of Parties."

38. James Madison, "Who Are the Best Keepers of the People's Liberties?," Founders Online, December 20, 1792, http://founders.archives.gov/documents/Madison/01-14-02-0384.

39. James Madison, "Public Opinion," Founders Online, December 19, 1791, http://founders.archives.gov/documents/Madison/01-14-02-0145.

40. Thomas Jefferson, "I. Thomas Jefferson's Explanations of the Three Volumes Bound in Marbled Paper (the So-Called 'Anas')," Founders Online, February 4, 1818, https://founders.archives.gov/documents/Jefferson/03-12-02-0343-0002.

41. Madison, "A Candid State of Parties."

42. Martin Van Buren, "Autobiography," in *Annual Report of the American for the Year 1918*, *Vol.* 2, ed. John C. Fitzpatrick (Washington, DC: Government Printing Office, 1920), 125.

Chapter 8. The Judiciary

1. This chapter draws on a larger debate about the role of politics in evaluating the meaning of the Constitution—and by implication the place of judicial review. On these issues, reasonable and intelligent people disagree. My agenda here is not to take sides

in this debate per se, although I am partial to the idea of a minimal role for the Supreme Court, which I do claim in this chapter is closer to a Madisonian view of the Constitution. Rather, my intent is to assert that, as the Court largely sits outside the political process, it is not as bound by the constitutional mandate of consensus. This has enabled the Court in some instances to successfully settle fraught social disputes, but in other cases, it has undermined the efforts of the political branches to reach compromises that reflect public opinion. For some excellent entries in the debate of the Court in political life, see Randy E. Barnett, *Our Republican Constitution: Securing the Liberty and Sovereignty of We the People* (New York: Broadside Books, 2016); Mark Tushnet, *Taking the Constitution Away from the Courts* (Princeton, NJ: Princeton University Press, 1999); and Greg Weiner, *The Political Constitution: The Case Against Judicial Supremacy* (Lawrence, KS: Kansas University Press, 2019).

2. James Madison, "Establishment of Inferior Courts," Founders Online, June 5, 1987, https://founders.archives.gov/documents/Madison/01-10-02-0018.

3. Max Farrand, ed., *The Records of the Federal Convention* (New Haven, CT: Yale University Press, 1966), 1:124.

4. *Federalist*, no. 78 (Alexander Hamilton).

5. National Archives, "The United States Constitution: A Transcription," https://www.archives.gov/founding-docs/constitution-transcript.

6. *Federalist*, no. 78 (Hamilton).

7. Philip B. Kurland and Ralph Lerner, eds., "Brutus, No. 11," in *The Founders' Constitution* (Chicago: University of Chicago Press, 1986): 1:282.

8. James Madison, "Removal Power of the President," Founders Online, June 18, 1789, https://founders.archives.gov/documents/Madison/01-12-02-0146.

9. *Federalist*, no. 26 (Alexander Hamilton).

10. James Madison, "The Report of 1800," Founders Online, January 7, 1800, https://founders.archives.gov/documents/Madison/01-17-02-0202.

11. James Madison, letter to Charles J. Ingersoll, June 25, 1831, Founders Online, https://founders.archives.gov/documents/Madison/99-02-02-2374.

12. Thomas Jefferson, letter to Abigail Adams, September 11, 1804, Founders Online, https://founders.archives.gov/documents/Adams/99-03-02-1317.

13. Jefferson, letter to Adams.

14. *United States v. Butler*, 297 US 1, 79 (1936) (Stone, J., dissenting), https://supreme.justia.com/cases/federal/us/297/1.

15. Abraham Lincoln, "First Inaugural Address of Abraham Lincoln," Yale Law School, Lillian Goldman Law Library, Avalon Project, https://avalon.law.yale.edu/19th_century/lincoln1.asp.

16. US Const. amend. XIV, § 1.

17. *Federalist*, no. 84 (Alexander Hamilton).

18. Quoted in David M. O'Brien and Gordon Silverstein, *Constitutional Law and Politics: Struggles for Power and Governmental Accountability* (New York: W. W. Norton and Company, 2020), 35.

Chapter 9. Constitutional Virtue

1. Niccolò Machiavelli, *Discourses on Livy*, ed. Bernard Crick (New York: Penguin Books, 2003), 385–86.

2. Martin Van Buren, "Autobiography," in *Annual Report of the American for the Year 1918, Vol. 2*, ed. John C. Fitzpatrick (Washington, DC: Government Printing Office, 1920), 125.

3. *Federalist*, no. 55 (James Madison).

4. *Federalist*, no. 10 (James Madison).

5. James Madison, "Judicial Powers of the National Government," Founders Online, https://founders.archives.gov/documents/Madison/01-11-02-0101.

6. Michael Scherer, "Barack Obama's 'Enemies,'" *Time*, November 1, 2010, https://swampland.time.com/2010/11/01/barack-obamas-enemies.

7. Brian Montopoli, "Romney to Campaign Donors: Obama Voters 'Dependent,' See Selves as 'Victims,'" CBS News, September 17, 2012, https://www.cbsnews.com/news/romney-to-campaign-donors-obama-voters-dependent-see-selves-as-victims.

8. Katie Reilly, "Read Hillary Clinton's 'Basket of Deplorables' Remarks About Donald Trump Supporters," *Time*, September 10, 2016, https://time.com/4486502/hillary-clinton-basket-of-deplorables-transcript.

9. Amie Parnes, "Biden Fails to Break GOP 'Fever,'" *Hill*, June 14, 2021, https://thehill.com/homenews/administration/558065-biden-fails-to-break-gop-fever.

10. Theodore Roosevelt, "A Confession of Faith," Ohio State University, eHistory, August 6, 1912, https://ehistory.osu.edu/exhibitions/1912/1912documents/a_confession_of_faith.

11. *Federalist*, no. 10 (Madison).

12. Thomas Jefferson, "First Inaugural Address, March 4, 1801," Founders Online, https://founders.archives.gov/documents/Jefferson/01-33-02-0116-0004.

13. Library of Congress, "James Monroe to General Andrew Jackson, December 14, 1816, from Correspondence of Andrew Jackson," https://tile.loc.gov/storage-services/service/mss/maj/01043//01043_0104_0125.pdf.

14. Henry Clay, "On the Seminole War, January 1819," in *The Speeches of Henry Clay*, ed. Calvin Colton (New York: A. S. Barnes and Company, 1857), 1:181.

Conclusion

1. *Federalist*, no. 39 (James Madison).

2. James Madison, "Popular Election of the First Branch of the Legislature," Founders Online, https://founders.archives.gov/documents/Madison/01-10-02-0021.

3. Max Farrand, ed., *The Records of the Federal Convention of 1787* (New Haven, CT: Yale University Press, 1966), 3:642–43.

Index

Printed in the USA
CPSIA information can be obtained
at www.ICGtesting.com
JSHW011441250923
49098JS00015B/188/J